The Witness

Dr. Charles R. Vogan Jr.

Copyright © 1998 Charles R. Vogan Jr.
All rights reserved

Scripture taken from the HOLY BIBLE, NEW INTERNATIONAL VERSION,
Copyright © 1973, 1978, 1984 International Bible Society. Used by permission of Zondervan Bible Publishers.

ISBN 978-0-6151-3863-3

Ravenbrook Publishers

A subsidiary of
Shenandoah Bible Ministries

www.shenbible.org

Contents

Introduction	3
What is a Witness?	9
What Do They Witness About?	47
The Witness of the Spirit	77
The Witness of Christ	112
The Witness of the Prophets	143
The Witness of the Father	168
The Witness of the Apostles	186
Hostile Witnesses	215
The Witness of the Church	241
Conclusion	258

Introduction

In our present age, the things of God – especially the kinds of things that we find in the Bible – are usually dismissed as so much nonsense. Many people simply don't believe what they hear about the Christianity that generations of former saints have found so much consolation, strength, and encouragement in. Instead, they have found new experts who claim to be able to show us the truth about ourselves and world we live in – *without* using the Bible. Science, psychology, sociology, our new culture, education, the new sophistication of the 20th-century man – all these things make it almost impossible for someone to believe the simple Gospel.

On the other hand, the Bible very emphatically teaches that the spiritual world of God is real. There *are* such things as holiness and righteousness, punishment and reward, the throne of God and the soul of man. Jesus really is the Son of God, and anybody who doesn't believe that will most definitely die in their sins with no hope of eternal life. (John 8:24) And the picture it paints is drastically different from the one we get from our modern experts. We are facing a crisis of authority.

But in our age, it seems to be the fashion to believe one's senses, and the hard results of scientific investigation – but not any religious claims. You may not have thought about this much, but what that means is this: if we don't believe the Bible anymore, we are actually calling someone a *liar*. That may seem terrible, but it's true. And since the Bible is God's book, anybody who doesn't believe that it's the truth is really accusing God himself of being a liar.

> Anyone who does not believe God has made him out to be a liar, because he does not believe the *testimony* God has given about his Son. (1 John 5:10)

God is no fool; he doesn't leave himself vulnerable to the attacks of ignorant and wicked men. They may deny that he exists, and they may despise who he is; but at some point the Lord *will* prove to them that they were dead wrong about him. He has a secret weapon that destroys all of their arguments: **the witness**.

In other words, the Bible, and even the church, backs up all of its claims with eyewitnesses, people who have seen and experienced what they are telling us about God. They didn't make up this business of Christianity! The Lord very wisely made sure that there would be witnesses of his work on Earth, so that anybody who heard their testimony would have to *deny that the witness saw it* in order to reject it. And that, as you will find even in a court of law, let alone before God's judgment seat, is a risky argument at best, and foolishness at worst.

A witness is a special person in God's kingdom. Everything that God does on Earth is witnessed by someone, so that he or she can relay that information on to others. We all need to know what the witnesses have seen about God; our future hangs on this information. Therefore, to accept the testimony of an eyewitness pleases God, and to reject it is to reject God himself.

> If the world hates you, keep in mind that it hated me first. If you belonged to the world, it would love you as its own. As it is, you do not belong to the world, but I have chosen you out of the world. That is why the world hates you. Remember the words I spoke to you: 'No servant is greater than his master.' If they persecuted me, they will persecute you also. If they obeyed my teaching, they will obey yours also. They will treat you this way because of my Name, for they do not know the One who sent me. (John 15:18-21)

Introduction – 5

Often our very salvation depends on whether we believe the words of a witness. As Jesus said once, if people don't believe the testimony of the man who saw the acts of God (in other words, an eyewitness), they won't believe in God even if another miracle is performed just for them (Luke 16:31). That is, since they refuse to believe the witnesses whom God sent to them with his message, he certainly isn't going to do anything more for them – it would be useless. To God, the witness was sufficient proof. His testimony is enough to convict them.

But if we believe the testimony of a witness, we are opening ourselves to the vast riches of what God can and will do for his people – because that's what the witnesses are really showing us. Their testimony is convincing proof that knowing God is rewarding, that Christianity does make a difference in one's life, and (the other side of the coin) that turning your back on God is going to prove disastrous in the end. In other words, there really is a God, and he really is like the Bible (which is nothing less than the testimony of eyewitnesses) describes him.

The purpose of the Bible is to reveal God to us. No other book can do that, because only God can reveal himself, and he chose to do it through the Bible. Everything in it centers on God in some way. And the eyewitness is God's special strategy that he uses throughout the book – this is the scheme that he devised to convince man of his reality. An eyewitness provides an irrefutable argument to his opponents: there are no loopholes, there is no escape from the spiritual point that he's pressing on us. If we study this testimony then we will know the truth about God, we will know his ways, we will know his works that he does in this world that affect us.

It's probably the most effective way of making his point that he could possibly have used. For that reason, we can't list here all the separate testimonies that are in the Bible because *the entire Bible* is a testimony to God. The whole book witnesses to the reality and nature of the Lord. Of course there are many ways that the Bible uses to teach us about God, but it helps us to understand what the actual nature of the Bible really is if we want to see it in its true light: an eyewitness account of the reality of God.

If we accept the fact that the Bible is a collection of testimonies from eyewitnesses, then that puts a whole new light on God's Word. **First**, it puts authority back into the Bible. In our age we pretty much have rejected the Bible's authority; we don't really think that it contains the truth for our new generation. Even Christians are guilty of this, because they often look to other sources for their authority (for example, science, psychology, secular education, politics, etc.) instead of to the Bible.

If the Bible were only another philosophy among many, we could easily accept or reject it according to our own feelings and opinions. But since it's a testimony from eyewitnesses, there is no way we can reject it. We can't doubt what the witnesses have seen and heard. What the Bible says about God is true and urgent. Each generation has to come to grips with the truth of the Bible because our lives depend on it. The Bible is discussing matters that we can't afford to ignore:

> The Bible shows us the authority of the *Creator*, the Provider, the God who made and cares for the world on a daily basis. We owe him for everything that we have. Since we depend on him so completely, it's wise to learn how to fear him, to trust in him, to wait on him, to look to him for everything that we need. Any act that would make this God angry with us is foolishness.

> We see also in the Bible the *salvation* that we need from our sins. We are all marked to die, because of the treasonable sins that we have committed against the Creator. But in Jesus we see the picture of one who has come to save us from sin and death; he reaches down to us and calls us by name in order to save us. If we reject this, we reject our last hope for life.

> We see also in the Bible a warning of impending *judgment* – the last day when God will get all the glory that he fully deserves, and we will be examined for what we really are. On that day there will be no more

appeals, there will be no more chance to change. The judge will pronounce his judgment over us, to the satisfaction of all present, and we will get what we fully deserve. In light of that day, we ought to be taking God and his demands upon us more seriously.

If these things are true, it makes the Bible the most valuable treasure that we have in this life. It is literally our key into the secrets of eternal life. As an eyewitness account, we must accept the message of the Bible as it stands – with no changes, with full confidence in what it says, and even in the *way* it says it. This is the truth, no matter what people in our generation might say about it.

Second, it puts depth into the message of the Bible. There is more truth in what it has to say about God, about us, and about the world than we realize. Science, for example, for as much as it has helped modern man, has done him a great disservice: it has made him skeptical of any system of truth that's not verifiable by the scientific method. That means that we have even become skeptical about God. But God's eyewitnesses testified to a spiritual reality that scientists can't conceive of, and can't measure with their instruments. Are we free to call that witness a liar because science can't verify his statements? Or does this mean that there's a bigger reality than the physical world, with meaning and purpose beyond the reach of scientific instruments?

God's witnesses have seen a huge world out there beyond our physical senses. It's a world where God rules, where holiness and righteousness are the standards of the kingdom, where the wicked are destroyed and the children of God welcomed into eternal dwellings. All this is quite real, the eyewitnesses tell us, even though none of the rest of us can see it. In other words, what the Bible has to say is actually a better way of describing God's creation than the current sterile system that science has given us. There are many holes in our present scientific worldview that the Bible can fill in for us; and there are outright lies that we have believed from the world system that the Bible intends to correct.

So, in God's great wisdom he has provided eyewitness accounts to prove his reality and glory. It's our duty to listen to them, believe them, and act on what they tell us. Only in this way will we be using the Bible as God intended us to.

> But these are written that you may believe that Jesus is the Christ, the Son of God, and that by believing you may have life in his Name. (John 20:31)

What is a Witness?

Though we often think of a witness in a courtroom, a witness is actually important in all aspects of life. Every culture depends on the testimony of witnesses in some way. Without the testimony of eyewitnesses, not only would we not get the daily news, but we would not be able to pass on what we've learned from one generation to the next. We may or may not believe everything we're told, but we at least like to hear what others have seen so that we can make our own judgment.

The need for truth

But first let's examine the reason we need witnesses: the human mind requires *facts* about its surroundings. We need knowledge, because all of our actions and feelings are based on what we learn by our senses. For example, if we're about to go outside, we need to know what the weather is like so that we can wear the appropriate clothing. What is frustrating, however, is when we can't get reliable information. If we can't find out the truth, we don't know the right thing to do or we may end up doing the wrong thing. When the weatherman tells us it's going to be a warm and sunny day, and we get caught in the rain instead, we aren't very likely to trust his word again in the future!

We value the truth so highly that we're willing to pay for it. Newspapers bring it to our doorstep every day; radio and TV are also primary sources for truth. Our educational institutions train the young with (supposedly) the truth during their formative years. As one example of our jealousy for the truth: when a book is published that is just a made-up story, we insist that the word "fiction" appear on the cover.

We punish those who lie to us. Government agencies police the marketing business for dangerous "false advertising." Courts slap fines on those who perjure themselves and lie under oath. Words like "hypocrite" and "fake" show our true feelings toward those who prove to be false and untrustworthy.

Obviously, if you think about our society and the many ways that we get, rely on, and test for truth, we all prize truth above most other things. We value and need the truth, so that we can make intelligent decisions and act on them with some kind of certainty that things will turn out as we hope. Truth makes life work.

There are more important issues in life than the weather, however. We need some serious questions answered about our world and what we are doing in it. What do we need to know about?

We want the truth about ourselves: What is man, really? Is he just an animal, or does he have a soul? What are we here for? Are we basically good or bad, morally speaking? Are we morally responsible to anybody? Can we put together a perfect life here on earth? Or are we incapable of doing anything good? Is sin really sin? Or is it a cultural matter that changes from generation to generation? Has a person achieved happiness when he has achieved his personal goals, and when he is at peace with himself and his neighbor? Or is there something more that we have to do? Or is our life as low as the animals and nothing matters more than to eat, drink, and find pleasure in whatever one does?

We want the truth about the universe: Is the world what the scientists say it is – just matter and energy that has been here forever and will continue forever? Are we all part of a mindless cosmic dance in which we play our little part in history and then eventually disappear as evolution has its purposeless way? Is reality limited to what we can see and hear and touch – or is there a bigger spiritual reality beyond our senses? What happens to a person when he dies? Is it dust returning to dust, or does the spirit fly to another world where there is judgment and just reward?

We want the truth about God: The biggest question ever posed by man is this: Is there a God? If he really exists, what is he like? What does he think of us? How much of a part does he play in our lives? Do his actions take priority over ours – in other words, are we helplessly living out his eternal plans? Or does he give us the free will to override his own purposes if we wish? What is his definition of sin? Why does this God, if he exists, allow the appalling suffering of mankind throughout history? Will he reward all of mankind, or are there some whom he simply can't tolerate? Finally, if God doesn't exist, why then do we keep returning to the subject?

If this is how valuable truth is to us, then we also must find a way to make sure we get the truth and nothing but the truth. Any lie, any unreliable information that someone passes to us, has the potential of ruining something: either our reputation, or our plans, or our friendships, or our safety, or even our civilization. There has to be some reliable way of getting the truth, and making sure that it's the truth. Too much is at stake here to not be sure.

A witness

Fortunately there is a way of making sure that we get truth and not lies. What we do is rely on *the testimony of someone who saw what happened.* When we need the truth, it's time to turn to the witness.

The witness saw it – Simply put, a witness is someone who saw or heard an event that the rest of us were not there to see. The witness was present when it happened; he experienced it firsthand. For instance, people who have been present at the launch of a space shuttle can relive the moment in a way that the rest of us can only poorly imagine, because the experience was so breathtakingly unique. The only way we can fully know what they felt is if we were there to experience it for ourselves. But since most of us will never have the opportunity to experience it, we can only take the word of the eyewitness if we want to learn what it was like.

A witness also plays an important role in the courtroom. When someone has been accused of a crime, he must appear in court and defend himself. Usually a defendant claims to be innocent; but since we can't just take someone's word for things (because he will more often than not lie in order to stay out of trouble!), we must have some other way of finding out the truth. People are incurable liars, and they have no problem telling a lie if it means that they will stay out of trouble. So we have a prosecuting attorney, and a judge, and a jury to decide the case. Hopefully between the three of them, the court will be able to find out what really happened. But what makes a courtroom argument more convincing is if there was a witness present at the scene. He claims to have been there; he saw whether the defendant did the crime in question. Based on his testimony, the accused will either be acquitted or condemned.

The witness knows the details – The witness tells us details of what happened that we wouldn't otherwise know. We can know in general what happened, but the witness can give us a step-by-step account of the event. He can separate out the important facts from the unimportant ones. He tells us a story that fascinates us, because it fascinated him. He fills in the gaps of our knowledge with details and relationships. All these details are important to us, because based on those facts, we can make informed decisions. So the witness becomes a valuable source of information for us.

The witness tells us how to read the evidence – Physical evidence can often be used for or against an argument in the courtroom; therefore it's not always trustworthy. But a witness is like us. He uses the same senses that we have, and he knows the certainty of a fact just as well as we would know it. Without a witness, physical evidence can be presented to support just about anybody's argument; but because the witness testifies to what he saw, we now look at the evidence in only one way – as it illustrates his testimony. Even if what he says contradicts the evidence (which sometimes happens), we often have no choice but to believe his testimony. Physical evidence can be so misleading that we sometimes have to distrust the conclusions it makes us jump to, when a witness contradicts it. That's how important an eyewitness is in court.

The Bible's witnesses

We can expect that the Bible would use witnesses in a unique way. Biblical witnesses aren't interested in just any event; what they testify about is a reality that people have never been able to figure out on their own. The Biblical witnesses have been sent to us to convince us about the most important question that mankind has ever struggled with:

**These witnesses have seen or experienced
the reality of God.**

What this means is that they can clear up many spiritual questions that we have not been able to solve on our own. For example, is there a God? What is this God like? What does he do, and what does he not do? What are his plans for his world, and for us? What does he expect of us? If we have the right answers for these questions, that means we will experience a peace in our lives that God intended when he first made us, a peace that comes with knowing and trusting in this God. But with the wrong answers, we can only expect to have pain, frustration, and hardship in life. Getting the right answers, therefore, is extremely important to us. That's why we need this testimony from the eyewitnesses of God.

> **Philosophies and religions have failed:** The philosophies and religions of this world have tried and failed to satisfy the longings of man's soul. None of them (if they ignore the Bible) give us the truth. We know this because they disagree with other each other in so many ways. If they *were* the truth, there should be some kind of agreement; but since there are so many contradictory views in man's religious systems, someone must be missing the point. Also, none of these philosophies and religions satisfactorily explain our world. When we try to use them in practical ways, we quickly find their weaknesses: the so-called truths break down at some point because they don't fit reality. Many people have put their trust in false religions and lived to regret their choice.
>
> **God is wrapped in mystery:** There's another problem that these world-views have struggled with, another reason that they can't put their finger on the truth: God himself is a mysterious being. He hides himself in such a way that it's not easy, in fact it's impossible, to find out what he's really like unless he reveals himself on purpose. God is invisible, his ways are far above our ways, and he doesn't do things the way we do. This means that what he does is often incomprehensible to us. What he thinks and plans is far beyond our finding out. God is spiritual, and we are physical; how can flesh and blood possibly hope to understand the spiritual world?
>
> **We have offended God:** As if these problems weren't enough, we have offended God by breaking

his laws repeatedly since our birth. God set his Law over his new Creation at the beginning. But we turned our backs on him: we chose to rule ourselves instead of submit to his rule. Since God is offended, it's no wonder that he stays away, far enough that we will never hope to know him personally. A holy, offended God is not going to come close and be friendly on our terms. If he feels the need to tell us something about himself, he will be selective in his revelation: he has his own reasons for giving this information to certain people and not to others. In other words, if we hope to know God, it won't be because we were able to figure him out, or were able to find the door to Heaven and open it ourselves. God must open it from his side.

So, since we don't and can't know God on our own, we need a reliable source of information on God – something that we can depend on, something that will accurately reflect who he is, something that will put us in touch with him. The Bible fits the specifications remarkably. The reason the Bible proves itself over and over, and the reason that it turns out to be so dependable under so many different circumstances, is because it consists of the *testimony* of many witnesses who have themselves experienced the reality of God. There is no arguing against a successful method. Testimony is an amazingly simple way of proving a point that no other method can hope to achieve. There is simply no argument against it.

The reality of God is the biggest question of our times. Of course unbelievers don't believe in God, or anything of the spiritual world. But even Christians sometimes act as if there is no God. When they don't pray for anything in particular, when they rely upon themselves to solve problems, when they show no fear of a holy God and live in sin, then it's obvious they don't believe in the God that they talk about. Also, when the Bible teaches us about the things that God does, we usually don't believe it. It doesn't fit in with our modern world-view, therefore we think it can't be true. For example, the Bible tells us that God does his work through miracles – but in our scientific age, that's a difficult idea to believe in. The modern man has basically talked himself out of the idea of miracles – except for what science can do for him.

That's where the witness comes in. He testifies that what we read in the Word is true; he saw it himself. Now we're faced with a two-pronged argument that's almost impossible to argue with: first the Bible reveals God to us, and then the witness comes along and testifies that he himself saw God and his works firsthand and can verify that it's all true. Our natural unbelief rebels at the truth of the Bible, but we can't ignore both the Word *and* the witness without calling them both liars – which is a fool's argument.

There are certain characteristics about witnesses that make them invaluable to us, and unique.

- **A witness is *reliable*.** We like reliability, because we want to know the truth about things. Scientists, for example, have often said that if someone can show them a photograph of a ghost then they'll believe in them! The camera will generally show us what is really there (though there is such a thing as trick photography!), and that's why they are so valuable. But when it comes to spiritual matters, these are things that scientific instruments will never be able to measure. In fact, there is nothing on earth that can prove the reality of God. How then can we know whether God really exists, or that any event of history was the result of God working among us? Can we trust the claims of religion? So much is at stake here that we can't use anything less than a reliable witness.

    A witness claims to have seen real things; it's not his imagination, a myth, hearsay, tradition, the workings of a fevered mind, or anything else that can and should be challenged by skeptics. He has truly seen God – or experienced the hand of God in his life. And if that really happened to him, then God expects us to believe his testimony. We are dangerously close to alienating ourselves from God when we doubt the word of his witnesses. For instance, when the angel Gabriel came to tell Zechariah that his wife would give birth to John the Baptist, Zechariah wanted some proof that such a impossible thing would really happen. The angel's response was predictable!

> I am Gabriel. *I stand in the presence of God*, and I have been sent to speak to you and to tell you this good news. And now you will be silent and not able to speak until the day this happens, because you did not believe my words, which will come true at their proper time. (Luke 1:19-20)

Gabriel came with God's very words, and it was a foolish thing for Zechariah to doubt that the angel was accurately representing God. If we doubt that someone has seen the president of our country, for example, that's a small matter. But if someone claims to have seen or heard God, we need to walk carefully here – God sent them to us for a reason, and our correct response is to hear and obey. For example, Gamaliel, who sat with others in judgment on the Apostles, understood the need for caution in a case where the witness claims to have seen God:

> Therefore, in the present case I advise you: Leave these men alone! Let them go! For if their purpose or activity is of human origin, it will fail. But if it is from God, you will not be able to stop these men; you will only find yourselves fighting against God. (Acts 5:38-39)

- This leads us to the next point: **a witness is telling us the *truth*.** Either he has seen God, or heard the words of God, but in either case we have no right to doubt what he is saying. This is why, after all, we have a witness in the first place – so that we can *know the truth*. Since everyone has his own opinion on things, it's no wonder that there are all sorts of theories about what God is really like. Nobody really likes what the Bible says about him; many prefer to believe in false gods who will let us do whatever sin we want.

But the witness puts all the arguments to rest. What he saw and experienced, we *have* to believe, even if it contradicts our opinions, even if it doesn't make any sense to us. He saw the true God and can tell us exactly what God is like. There is just no room for doubt or opinions when an eyewitness has spoken. For example, the Pharisees couldn't argue with the facts about Jesus' miracles. Not only did they themselves witness many of these miracles, but they also got to interview other witnesses. All this made them very uncomfortable about Jesus, but they couldn't deny any of it – they were trapped by the truth.

> "We know that God spoke to Moses, but as for this fellow, we don't even know where he comes from." The man answered, "Now that is remarkable! You don't know where he comes from, yet he opened my eyes. We know that God does not listen to sinners. He listens to the godly man who does his will. Nobody has ever heard of opening the eyes of a man born blind. If this man were not from God, he could do nothing." (John 9:29-33)

Since a witness of God tells us the truth, we have to start there and let it shape what we believe, even if it means changing what we have believed in the past. For example, another "hotspot" in today's circles is what to believe about Creation. Interestingly, we do have a witness of the event – the Holy Spirit was there during the entire process, and he testifies to us what happened and how it happened. His testimony, however, flies in the face of all modern science and "common sense." So who will we believe? If God's key witness contradicts our opinions, there is only one thing for a man of faith to do – change his own opinions in favor of the Holy Spirit's eyewitness account. The Spirit is telling us *the truth*; God's witnesses cannot lie.

- Finally, **a witness is specially *qualified* to do his/her job.** That is, they have a calling, a mission, to convey information about God to others. You have heard of "key witnesses" in court cases who were the only ones on the scene, and who are called to testify about what happened; the case can't be made without their input. If something should happen to the key witness, the case folds. Likewise, in God's scheme of things, witnesses who testify about God and his works are key to our faith: based on their testimony, we can have faith, we can know the truth about God and ourselves, we can *know* what course of action to take in our own lives to please God.

These key witnesses came at critical times in Israel's history, and in the history of the Church, so that they could bring the people of God face to face with the reality of God. God gave them only the revelation that the rest of us needed to hear, and the perfect opportunity – time, place, and audience – to proclaim it. That is, God set everything up so that the witness was in a perfect position for the job. The Apostles, for example, were chosen to testify to the world about the things they saw in Jesus: "He appointed twelve – designating them Apostles – that they might be with him and that he might send them out to preach and to have authority to drive out demons." (Mark 3:14-15) Without the testimony of the Apostles, we would have no Scriptures, and we would have no Church. Their witness is foundational to the Kingdom of God:

> Consequently, you are no longer foreigners and aliens, but fellow citizens with God's people and members of God's household, built on *the foundation of the Apostles and Prophets*, with Christ Jesus himself as the chief cornerstone. (Ephesians 2:19-20)

The primary strategy

In the war between truth and lies, the most important, and the most effective, weapon that God uses is the eyewitness. It's the one unarguable reality that man (and the devil) can't resist or deny. Of course God uses other methods to build his Kingdom, but the strategy of using a witness is so overwhelmingly convincing and effective that the Lord used it from the beginning of Bible history to the end.

Testimony achieves the goals that God is after. He isn't interested only in spreading some knowledge around, as if people can gather it up in a book and store it in a library. God's purpose is to convict people of serious matters – issues that we remain hardened, obstinate, and rebellious about. He wants a change of heart: he wants rebellious sinners to lay down their arms, repent of all the wickedness they did against him, and willingly take on his Name and live in his Kingdom according to his rules. God wants the truth to reign in this world for a change; he's tired of the lies about him. Darkness and ignorance only promotes the devil's purposes and destroys the creation that God made at the beginning. God wants to destroy the kingdom of darkness and ignorance, suffering and sin, frustration and rebellion that the devil created – and set up a new Kingdom of righteousness, life, light, peace and justice.

All this is a high purpose, and it will require the most powerful tools and weapons that Heaven possesses. We can tell, therefore, how much confidence that God has in any particular weapon when he relies on it so heavily in the war.

That should tell us something about the strategy of his using witnesses throughout the Bible. The entire Bible is a collection of eyewitness testimonies to God and his world of the Spirit. Not only were there witnesses in every era of Biblical history, but their testimony takes many forms. These are some of the different forms of testimony used:

- **Ark of the Testimony** – The ark that was in the Temple was the place where God sat among his people. It was his throne, and the Israelites went there to speak to him and get blessings from him. Amazing things happened there at the ark! It was plain to the Israelites that there was a living God sitting among them.

- **Prophets** – These men saw the King of kings in his holiness, and heard his condemnation of the wickedness of the kingdoms of the earth. They heard the Lord's secret counsel against the wicked, and saw the Lord send his hosts against the wicked to destroy them and set up a righteous kingdom in their place.

- **History** – It's not someone's runaway imagination that the amazing events that led Abraham to Canaan, and the Israelites out of Egypt to the Promised Land, and the Jews into Exile and back again, were the hand of God. God led his people in plain ways (and explained what he was doing through their own testimony that we now have recorded for us in the Bible) so that he could make them his own people. And then he used them to testify to the rest of the world what life is like living in the presence of God.

- **Worship experiences** – The Temple of Israel wasn't like the temples of the heathen. God was there in person, and that's the only way we can explain the events that happened. The Lord on occasion filled his Temple so overwhelmingly that the priests couldn't go inside; they found forgiveness for sin there; the fire and cloud of the Tabernacle led the Israelites during their wanderings in the desert. We have eyewitness accounts for all these encounters between God and man.

- **Hostile witnesses** – This is such an effective way to challenge and destroy the arguments of those who deny God. There were those in Bible times also who didn't believe in God, and who didn't like what they heard about Israel's God. But they themselves saw him. They can testify (however unwillingly) that they saw this God, and he really is what the believers said about him.

- **Written records** – The Bible is a written record of the meeting between God and man. It isn't just a system of religion or philosophy, written at the leisure of intellectuals for the entertainment of the faithful. The books of the Bible are historical documents with all the authority of accepted testimonials from people who were there when God revealed himself to his people. They are first-hand records, not second-hand or hand-me-down accounts – they would stand in a court of law today as material of primary importance to prove the case of God's existence.

- **Eyewitnesses of miracles** – And we can't forget that the most disconcerting and amazing claim ever made about God is that he performed miracles – not clever sleights of hand, or scientific marvels in an age when men wouldn't understand the science involved. No, the witnesses of God's works tell us that he did things that no scientist, or scientific principle, could ever explain. He avoided natural means and did what he wanted by command, by the power of the Spirit – completely circumventing natural means.

Notice that each form of testimony that comes from these witnesses points us to the reality of God, and shows us something about a spiritual world that we would not otherwise be able to know or even understand. Their testimony is invaluable for helping us accept the fact of the existence of God. Without it we would have no Christianity, no faith, no assurance of life beyond this one.

In all these different kinds of testimony, the one element that is common across the board is *the presence of the Holy Spirit*. We will see later the role that the Spirit plays in the testimony of all the Bible's witnesses. Here, though, we want to note several points: **first**, the Spirit is always the link between God and man. God is Spirit, and if physical man (with his physical senses) is to get in touch with this God and understand him at all, the Spirit has to step in and become the "interface" between them. The Spirit makes it possible for a person to see and know God. He also takes the realities of God and his world and opens them up – makes them available – to humans. We don't know how, but the Spirit is able to bypass our physical senses and make us aware of spiritual realities. **Second**, the Spirit does the convincing. Man is so hard-hearted, so blind, so limited to his physical senses and "common sense," that even if he hears the truth it makes no impression on his heart. What the Spirit does is crack the "heart of stone" and pour in the truth from Heaven. He makes sure the words don't remain just words, that they set the heart and mind on fire from Heaven and change us into believers. If the truth of the Bible has any effect on us at all, it's because the Spirit makes it work.

One result of the Spirit being behind all the testimony of the Bible is that all the witnesses agree with each other. Never before in human history have we had such an example of corroborative testimony. The Biblical witnesses testify of the same God who does the same kinds of things over thousands of years. Hardly any of these witnesses were personally known to each other; yet what they say about God and his works is so alike, so uniform, that we are forced to admit that they must have seen him. They all must have experienced the same God.

Even though there are differences in their testimony, almost all of those differences are due to the fact that they are looking at someone who is perfectly huge and can't be described from any one angle. God wears many hats, so to speak; if we think we have him figured out from one perspective, we have only begun to understand him. So many people have gone into error about who God is and what he's like by focusing on just one aspect of him. These many witnesses of God, however, show us God in many roles: first he is a Judge, then he is the Redeemer of Israel, then he is the Fear of Isaac, and next he's the terror of Egypt. We need this many-sided picture of God in order to get a *full* picture of him.

The amazing thing about the testimony of all these Biblical witnesses is that their testimony interlocks to give us a complete system. Imagine a house being built. A blueprint of the house gives the builders an idea of what the whole thing will look like when it's done. They know by this how to build each part, and when to build each part, and how to do the final assembly, in order to successfully complete it. In the same way, pieces of information that show us crucial information about God have been coming in from witnesses over thousands of years that reveal to us the overall plan that God has been implementing in history. It shows us not only what he's like (it takes thousands of years of human history to unfold the many-sided character of God), but also what he had planned for mankind – for the entire world, for that matter. It also makes sense to us now, those who have been watching the picture coming together, to see what is yet to come based on the information that we have so far. The witnesses have been drawing out the blueprint of God's eternal house for us. And it all fits together; each part needed the parts before and after, each section fits into the overall plan neatly and logically. And all this was done without any direct cooperation between most of the witnesses!

This answers all sorts of objections that unbelievers charge against the Bible – for example, that the Bible's message is purely a result of its culture and therefore is subject to change; that the Bible is only some men's opinions and not binding on everyone; that the experts of today can easily find faults in the naïve world-view of the Bible's time; that parts of the Bible are more important and useful than others, and other parts can be safely ignored. None of these objections can withstand the reality of the testimony of thousands of eyewitnesses, however: from a legal point of view, the Bible's argument will stand in court against any of these baseless charges that have been thrown at it for centuries.

If you think about it, however, you would realize that this is the only fail-safe way the Bible could have come together. Purely doctrinal or philosophical systems have come and gone in quick succession in man's history. The cultural world-views of past civilizations sound strange to our modern ears today. Science has drastically altered the way we view and use our world around us; and what's to come in the future that will make our present scientific expertise obsolete? So any religious system based on changing circumstances like these wouldn't stand the test of time. It's a mercy, therefore, that God based his truth on eyewitness accounts. God is the one unchanging thing in our changing world; he remains the same forever. And if they have seen him, all they had to do was describe to the rest of us what they saw. That story can't change from generation to generation. And it's exciting when we are able to meet that same God ourselves and confirm their testimony of him!

Why is a witness necessary?

We live in a world of history: events come and go, and time and space control our lives within certain constraints. Though some of us would like to, none of us can know and experience everything there is to see. Man's life span used to be hundreds of years, but now it's an average of 80 years – which means that we can only do so much before we die. Many of us don't even have the opportunity to travel to other parts of the world; we are tied down to staying close to home because of family or job or finances.

This is the main reason we rely on witnesses. Since none of us can be everywhere at once, we turn to others who have seen things that we would like to see and listen to their testimony. We depend on them; since we ourselves will never experience it, we value the experiences of others who can share with us.

This is especially true when it comes to experiences involving the Lord and his work. Everything in the Bible, for example, happened long ago, so that none of us now have a hope of seeing what it talks about. Wouldn't we love to sit at the feet of Jesus, like his disciples and others on the mountain, listening to his sermon! What one of us wouldn't have paid whatever it takes for a trip to Palestine while Jesus taught and performed miracles? But we can't hope for that now; it's over, Jesus is gone back to Heaven, and things are different now. That's why the testimony of those who were there is so valuable to God's people. Jesus knew the disadvantage we would have, we who come much later in history: "Because you [*that is, the disciples*] have seen me, you have believed; blessed are those who have not seen and yet have believed." (John 20:29)

There are other reasons for having a witness when it comes to the things of God:

- **We wouldn't believe it otherwise.** This is embarrassing but true. We are naturally unbelievers from birth when it comes to God. We only believe what we ourselves have seen, and it helps if we can touch it and measure it with scientific instruments. Otherwise we consider the Bible stories as so much myth and legend.

    Can we be so stupid? Isn't the Word of God enough? Isn't the voice from Heaven clear enough to get our attention? Evidently not! Nobody believes the Gospel, nobody believes the truth about God, unless they are forced to by evidence that they cannot reasonably deny. After all, the Pharisees saw Jesus do his miracles and heard his wisdom, and still they rejected him. This shows the utter obstinacy of the human heart.

    There are many reasons for people's lack of faith in God. *First*, we are natural skeptics: we've been trained for years by Satan *not* to believe what the Bible says. By now it's second nature to us. In order to believe the Bible, we would have to undergo a drastic change of heart, and have our minds completely remade (which is, in fact, what happens at conversion – see Romans 12:1-2). *Second*, we reserve the right to make our own judgment on things. We don't willingly swallow someone else's interpretations. *Third*, we are terrified that the God of the Bible would be real! Being sinners from birth, we love our sin, we hate righteousness, we are on the side of lies and darkness. A God of light, of holiness and righteousness and justice, would destroy our comfortable world! *Fourth*, we are so incorrigible that we will fight for our sin, and fight against God and his righteousness, all the way to the prison door. We are spiritual criminals to the core of our beings; there is nothing in God that we like, and like an unrepentant convict we will defy God to his face and insist on our "innocence" even though he can so easily convict us of sin.

What we need, then, is something that we can't deny, something that won't go away, something that shames us and puts God back in authority where he belongs as our Creator and Redeemer. We need an argument so strong, and so convincing, that it will force the hardest heart to confess that God is true and *we have all been living in lies*.

Bare doctrine about God doesn't impress us. Truth can wash over us in a sermon, in a Bible lesson, without so much as raising a trace of interest or fear or love in the God that the doctrine describes, however accurately. But when someone stands up and testifies that he *knows* how true that doctrine is because God did the thing in his own life, *then* we listen. Then it's both difficult to deny, and interesting to us. Then the truth forces us to the wall like an accuser, and all of our opinions and theories look hollow and useless. Then the doctrine changes into a life-giving promise and we want to experience it too.

There's a *fifth* reason we don't believe the truth that the Bible teaches: the natural world just doesn't work like that. The truths about God in the Word are, as far as this world is concerned, so impossible and contrary to common sense that we can't help but have doubts about them. How can such miracles have happened? How can God forgive a hardened sinner? How can God raise the dead? How can there be a Heaven and Hell that nobody can see? It doesn't make sense! Things just don't work like that in this world.

But that's the point: *God does the impossible.* If we could get whatever we needed from the world then we wouldn't need God to do it for us. But because there's no salvation in this world, no help at all here for the needs of our souls, we are forced to look to God who is outside of the world and therefore not constrained by what we consider "possible." There is where the testimony of a witness becomes invaluable. He tells us that the impossible happened: he saw it, he heard it, he experienced it. Let the experts deny it; but he *knows* it happened, as impossible as it sounds, because he was there when it happened.

- **We desperately need what the witness saw.** Remember, a witness has a role to play; he's a critical part of the dynamics of God's growing Kingdom. God sent him to us to convince us of the truth of the salvation that's in Christ, if we will only believe.

We aren't dealing with just history or philosophy here. Biblical witnesses aren't just entertaining us with slide shows of their trip into Heaven. The kingdom of God is about our future, about life and death, obedience and rebellion, reward and punishment. This is information that we desperately need. We can liken it to a court case in which someone is accused of murder, and there is only one witness who can prove that he is really innocent. That witness *must* come and testify! Otherwise the accused might be punished for a crime he didn't commit. He may even be put to death.

We can also put it this way: we have a house to build, and we are naturally ignorant about the best way to build it, or even where to build it. All around us are those who have tried to figure it out on their own, and their houses have collapsed, caught fire, or failed in some way. Will we also be stubborn in this and build our house in a way that suits our fancy? Or will we listen to witnesses who are ready to teach us the way?

Our houses – our lives, in other words, are at stake here. It's foolish to turn our backs on what reliable witnesses have to teach us.

> Therefore everyone who hears these words of mine and puts them into practice is like a wise man who built his house on the rock. The rain came down, the streams rose, and the winds blew and beat against that house; yet it did not fall, because it had its foundation on the rock. But everyone who hears these words of mine and does not put them into practice is like a foolish man who built his house on sand. The rain came down, the streams rose, and the winds blew and beat against that house, and it fell with a great crash. (Matthew 7:24-27)

- **The witness directs us to God.** We can know a faithful witness from a false witness in this one point. If someone says, in essence, "Look at me!" (and there are many ways to do this, both clever and stupid) then they aren't one of God's witnesses. The witnesses in God's employment all point to something about God, never to themselves.

God is what we really need, not more of man or this world. We have spent years of frustration trying to get what we need out of this world, and all we will have for our efforts when we die are memories of failures.

> This too is a grievous evil: As a man comes, so he departs, and what does he gain, since he toils for the wind? All his days he eats in darkness, with great frustration, affliction and anger. (Ecclesiastes 5:16-17)

But God provides miracles to overcome the obstacles of the world, wisdom that confounds the wisdom of ignorant men, and life where there has been only death. Once we see that our only hope is God, then we will begin looking for open doors into his presence. We will be looking for anybody who has concrete information about the Lord, and listening to whatever news we can get of him.

This fits in exactly with God's plans, because he desires the salvation of men. He won't let us grope in the darkness, never finding what we desire. He sends messengers who bring news about him. His faithful witnesses will point the way to life; they will show us the way to Heaven where we will find the Lover of our souls. Why would they want to draw attention to themselves, as if they had anything that a sinner needs? When the angels, for example, came to deliver the words of God to men, they repeatedly warned that it's forbidden to bow down to them and worship (though they were so bright and powerful that men felt impelled to bow down to them – for an example, see Revelation 19:10). The message was from God, and the person involved was expected to fear and worship God as a result – never the messenger.

Perhaps this is where Satan failed. He started out as one of the "sons of God" as the brightest of the angels. He loved the respect that he could get if he directed everyone's attention to himself instead of to God. What was Satan really doing when he tried to get others to look at him? **First**, he denied the glory that God deserves. God is the source of all good things, and the only one who rules the universe. To claim any good thing or ability apart from what God has given us is to deny him the preeminence in all things. **Second**, Satan pointed others away from life and salvation by pointing to himself. Our only hope is in God; by focusing on anything in this world other than God is to spend time among fools and husks instead of in the halls of God's Temple where the real treasures are. **Third**, Satan made himself appear as if he's the answer to man's dreams, as he was in control in this world. Of course that isn't true; Satan's so-called power is an empty promise, which anybody will find out if they make the mistake of taking what he offers. He uses his slaves and then throws them away when they're broken and empty. **Fourth**, in gaining man's attention and confidence, Satan cut off man's supply and communication line to Heaven. While listening to Satan and eating at his table, man didn't know that he lost his connection to God. In the process he lost his soul, since we can't live apart from God's presence.

Men would do well to learn a lesson from his fall. When we follow Satan's example and make people rely on us instead of God, we are literally cutting them off from their only hope in God. Such a burden on our consciences we don't need! For example, Paul cautions that young converts make poor leaders in the Church. "He must not be a recent convert, or he may become conceited and fall under the same judgment as the devil." (1 Timothy 3:6) The problem is that he will fall into pride too easily, when he sees how he can command respect and awe as he leads, and he will forget about what God's program is. He will steer people away from God, all the while claiming to lead them to God. Eventually everyone will realize that they've followed a fool out into the desert to die there. Their blood will be on his head.

We have another problem that a witness corrects. Our senses are so fixed on this world that we can't see spiritual realities. We think that life consists of eating, drinking, working and playing, and we hardly give a thought about what will happen when this life is over. Then the witness comes into our lives and opens up God's spiritual world, and we see new things there that we didn't know about: like God's utter holiness, our abysmal wickedness, the coming Kingdom that will destroy this world we live in, the wonders of Christ and the treasures in him that are free for those who come to him. Witnesses are messengers from another world, a world of permanence and overwhelming importance; their job is to convince us that we must "set your minds on things above, not on earthly things." (Colossians 3:2)

- **We become obligated to believe it.** Once the witness has spoken, we are in a different legal position than before we heard his testimony. Before, we were ignorant and didn't know what to believe or do about God; now, however, we *know* the truth and we are obligated to obey it. In many ways we have been told about our duty, about what the world is really like, about what God is like and what our hearts really are. Once we've been told about this, we are now responsible for what we know. Courts rely on this "you knew" principle and they can convict people on the basis of the fact that they did know the truth.

God does this on purpose. As we noted above, we aren't dealing with matters here that we can do without, or ignore if we please. The demands that God makes of us are legally binding: we have responsibilities that God gave us at Creation, we live as responsible citizens of his Kingdom, we are responsible to be holy according to the demands of his Law, we are duty-bound to give glory to God in all that we do and say. Judgment Day will be a sobering time for many people when they finally realize just how responsible they were in this world!

God's honor is at stake, at the very least, and he won't rest until we give an accounting to him for all the blessings that he showered on us through life. He created us to serve him; so he expects results, and he won't be happy if we try to plead ignorance when he has been telling us for years what he expects us to do to please him.

> That servant who knows his master's will and does not get ready or does not do what his

master wants will be beaten with many blows. But the one who does not know and does things deserving punishment will be beaten with few blows. From everyone who has been given much, much will be demanded; and from the one who has been entrusted with much, much more will be asked. (Luke 12:47-48)

Using a witness to make us accountable is a clever legal move on God's part. First he sends someone to us to tell us the truth. Now we have no excuse; on Judgment Day God will produce the very witness whom he sent to us, to repeat in the hearing of God's court what he told us – much to our shame and embarrassment. With the witness himself standing there, we will have no excuse or defense. We will realize then that the smart thing to do would have been to listen and believe it instead of doubt and reject it.

We know that "ignorance of the law is no excuse," though sometimes we think it's unfair that we have to find out the law for ourselves so that we don't get into trouble! But God isn't unfair about his Law: he has already sent us witnesses who testified of his spiritual world, and our responsibilities in it, so that we can't cry unfair on Judgment Day when he demands an accounting from us. We have all heard enough truth to make us accountable to him.

- **We need his testimony to form a correct judgment.** Consider a case in court. The defendant is accused of a crime, the state tries to argue in such a way as to convict him, and the defendant's lawyer tries to argue in such a way as to overturn the charge against him. The judge (or jury) listens to all this and has to decide what the truth is – not an easy job, since each party has their own interests at heart! Almost never do the two sides agree on the "facts."

Fortunately, the judge can call witnesses to the stand who can help. They saw what the defendant did or didn't do; they were there. They are under obligation to the court to tell the truth, so that the judge can find out what really happened. They are supposed to be impartial to either side and tell it like it is. From there, the judge can make a judgment (that's how he got his name!) about what really happened.

That's the same thing that witnesses of God do for us. They tell us the truth about God, about what they saw God do, and what happened in their own lives or the lives of others. Based on this crucial information, we can then make a judgment and start turning to God for those same things. Without that information we don't know what to do; when we have heard their testimony, however, the way to God becomes clear before us.

For example, let's say that we are considering how to worship God. What should we do? Can we go by our feelings, our own opinions, and worship God in ways that appeal to our senses and tastes? Do we have the freedom to do it as we please? Even when we read the Law with its strict requirements on worship, is that going to convince everyone? Wouldn't God allow us some freedom and creativity to worship him in new ways, if those new ways sound reasonable enough?

But there is a witness who saw what happened when someone decided to worship God in their own way, apart from the strict requirements of the Law:

> Aaron's sons Nadab and Abihu took their censers, put fire in them and added incense; and they offered *unauthorized* fire before the LORD, contrary to his command. So fire came out from the presence of the LORD and consumed them, and they died before the LORD. Moses then said to Aaron, "This is what the LORD spoke of when

he said: 'Among those who approach me I will show myself holy; in the sight of all the people I will be honored.'" (Leviticus 10:1-3)

Now you can theorize all you want about methods of worship, and whether God meant what he said in the Law about how to approach him. But this story, from those who saw it happen, should be a plain lesson for us all and leave no doubts about what we are responsible for. *God is not playing games.* He expects us to do what he commanded, in the *way* that he said to do it, or he will take drastic punitive action. And just because people have played games with him since then many times, and didn't get blasted for it on the spot, doesn't mean that God ignored their rebellion. "The Lord knows how ... to hold the unrighteous for the day of judgment, while continuing their punishment." (2 Peter 2:9) There are witnesses who can testify to that too.

On the other hand, some have found that when they obey God, they reap rich rewards. We like to see proofs of this because we get "weary in well-doing" and wonder if God really appreciates our faith and works of obedience. *He does.* We know this from witnesses who testified of his goodness. "God is not unjust; he will not forget your work and the love you have shown him as you have helped his people and continue to help them." (Hebrews 6:10) The disciples left home and jobs and became "fishers of men," who inherited the world, "sorrowful, yet always rejoicing; poor, yet making many rich; having nothing, and yet possessing everything." (2 Corinthians 6:10) We can believe their testimony that it *really is worth it* to leave the world, take up the cross, and follow Christ.

The only way to disprove it

There is only one way to prove that the testimony of an eyewitness is wrong – one has to show that he is *lying*. If someone successfully proves that the witness is lying, then suddenly the court brings its legal powers to bear upon the witness himself:

> The judges must make a thorough investigation, and if the witness proves to be a liar, giving false testimony against his brother, then do to him as he intended to do to his brother. You must purge the evil from among you. The rest of the people will hear of this and be afraid, and never again will such an evil thing be done among you. (Deuteronomy 19:18-20)

This shows the heavy responsibility laid on witnesses, and the supreme importance placed on their testimony. It must be accurate, true, and dependable.

So if someone challenges the witness, he has a big job on his hands. If he provides physical evidence to disprove the witness, the evidence has to be overwhelmingly convincing to the court. This might in fact work if the witness cannot claim to have seen the event clearly, having made no mistakes. If he only heard a rumor or saw what evidence was left after the event was over, then more convincing evidence could prove his testimony wrong. But if the witness saw the event in its entirety and can claim to know exactly what happened, then it is unlikely that any evidence offered contrary to his testimony will have much weight in court. Physical evidence has questionable value because it is usually open to so much interpretation — either side could easily use it to support its own argument.

This means, then, that to discount the testimony of a witness, the only option left is to call him a liar. Either the thing happened, or it did not. If it did not and the eyewitness claims that it did, then he is, simply put, a liar. And since the eyewitness is sworn to tell the truth, to call him a liar is a serious charge to make. One must have convincing proof in hand if he, wanting to accuse the witness of being a liar, does not want to incur the wrath of the court.

In order to disprove the stories of miracles in the Bible, we would have to call thousands of eyewitnesses liars. That would be the height of ignorance, arrogance and stupidity on our part. They were there; we were not. They saw it happen. Of course it was impossible, but that is why God had eyewitnesses on hand — we would not believe such things if people did not tell us that they saw them with their own eyes! It is not an argument against their testimony to say that we do not believe it. In God's court, the eyewitnesses have priority and carry the case. If we do not believe them, then we must show proof to God why they are lying. And it is also no argument that they were not scientifically astute enough to tell when a "miracle" was just a natural event. They are not claiming scientific proficiency; they are claiming that God did this miracle *apart from natural means*, which is the very point in question. Our challenge, to be plain, is to prove that God did not do it this way! Since we cannot imagine any way of producing results except through natural means, we have no hope of disproving the miracle. We are cornered into believing the witness.

No one can accuse the Spirit of telling a lie, or of not being scientifically astute. Man is desperately ignorant in comparison, and in the dark about God and his works, until the Spirit enlightens his mind and enables him to see the truth. The Spirit is literally our link to the truth. "But when he, the Spirit of truth, comes, he will guide you into all truth." (John 16:13) "And it is the Spirit who testifies, because the Spirit is the truth." (1 John 5:6) Truth is the way God looks at things, since he is the Creator and Judge of all things. But we certainly cannot know the mind of God unless the Spirit reveals it to us — which he does:

> The Spirit searches all things, even the deep things of God. For who among men knows the thoughts of a man except the man's spirit within him? In the same way no one knows the thoughts of God except the Spirit of God. (1 Corinthians 2:10-11)

Until the Spirit teaches us, we cannot know the truth about God and his works. That is why Jesus told Nicodemus, an expert in the Law of God, "I tell you the truth, no one can see the kingdom of God unless he is born again ... I tell you the truth, no one can enter the kingdom of God unless he is born of water and the Spirit." (John 3:3,5)

He is the expert witness. The Spirit was always called to testify when men needed to hear the truth about God. We find him present at many critical junctures in Biblical history, even in those situations when men were witnesses of God — they were enabled to see and know the presence of God through the work of the Spirit. Their ability to witness depended completely on the Spirit testifying to them of the reality of God.

We find this repeatedly in the Scriptures. David was filled with the Spirit and saw spiritual realities, which prompted all of his worship that is written in the Psalms. The Prophets saw, through the revelation of the Spirit, the realities of Heaven and the coming kingdom of God. The Apostles were filled with the Spirit and enabled to witness about Christ to the nations. John was filled with the Spirit when he received the revelation of Christ on Patmos. The Spirit has always been behind the testimony of human witnesses.

Therefore, to doubt the testimony of the Spirit is the greatest of sins. He is the fundamental source of all true knowledge of God. Jesus foretells disaster to the person who would call the Spirit a liar:

> I tell you the truth, all the sins and blasphemies of men will be forgiven them [*even, as we find in the parallel passage of Luke 12:10, sins against Christ himself*]. But whoever blasphemes against the Holy Spirit will never be forgiven; he is guilty of an eternal sin. (Mark 3:28-29)

The Spirit did not tell us the truth about God just to open himself to our foolish accusations against him — as if he is ignorant of scientific principles. Because the works of God are so important to our understanding of God, and God demands that we trust him in this, the Spirit himself testifies to his works. This is not a matter for trifling with the Almighty Creator. He purposely set up this situation in this way: we either believe his chosen witness, or we are in *legal* trouble with the Judge of Heaven and Earth.

Now we have come to the heart of the problem. At the risk of belaboring the issue, we have carefully taken up each point so that there is no mistaking what is at stake. Modern unbelievers purposely avoid talking about what they are, in fact, doing when they deny the facts of the Bible. We want to be very plain about this and pinpoint exactly what they are doing.

The only thing left to decide, therefore, is this: is the Bible true or not? As we have just seen, this is the same thing as saying — is the Spirit of God telling the truth *or is he lying*? When someone claims to be a witness, he is legally liable for what he says; ignorance or lack of scientific sophistication is not the issue. Someone's reputation (God's) is at stake, and a witness does not step up and take the stand lightly. And the event itself is of such a nature that either the thing happened as the witness claims or it did not happen. There are only two options available for us: either it is the truth or it is a bald lie.

It staggers the imagination to think that a human being, a sinner from birth, ignorant of so much truth, who can only know what his senses tell him and what has been told him by other ignorant humans, and who was born only yesterday compared to the ancient events of the Bible, would dare to call the Almighty God a *liar* about his own work. Yet that is exactly what is at issue here:

> Anyone who does not believe God has made him out to be *a liar*, because he has not believed the testimony God has given about his Son. (1 John 5:10)

When God himself (and that is who the Holy Spirit is) gives the testimony, our only safe recourse is to believe him. But people call him a liar all the time about the vast and convincing testimony that he has provided about Jesus Christ, as this passage shows. It is no wonder, then, that they also accuse him of lying about everything else that is taught in the Bible.

Modern unbelievers do not take the trouble to provide witnesses against God — because there are none. They are calling God a liar concerning the issues discussed in the Bible. They say it more politely than this, of course — they say that the stories are symbolic, that it's all open to interpretation, that the Bible is a charming myth and ancient folk literature. But the essence of what they are saying is that *they do not believe this testimony as it stands*. They do this in spite of the fact that God's creative work is always through miracles, that countless witnesses stand ready to testify to the reality of miracles, and that we can never know the truth of the matter unless we believe those whom God has sent to reveal this truth to us.

> And it is the Spirit who testifies, because the Spirit is the truth. For there are three that testify: the Spirit, the water and the blood; and the three are in agreement. We accept man's testimony, *but God's testimony is greater because it is the testimony of God*, which he has given about his Son. (1 John 5:6-9)

The Genesis account of Creation, at the very beginning of the Bible, is actually a test of our faith in the truthfulness of the Spirit throughout the rest of the Bible. If we cannot believe the sworn testimony of the Spirit about the first work of God in the world, then naturally we will not believe any of the testimonies that follow concerning the rest of his works. If we call God a liar about the greatest of his physical miracles, then we are hardly in a position to understand the greatest of his spiritual miracles — the redemption brought about by the Lord Jesus Christ. As this passage from 1 John shows, it is the same witness who testifies of both miracles.

Finally, for the determined doubter that questions why we should take the Spirit's testimony as the truth, we have only the challenge from Christ:

> If anyone chooses to do God's will, he will find out whether my teaching comes from God or whether I speak on my own. (John 7:17)

In other words, we cannot know for certain that what God says is true until we accept it wholeheartedly as *truth from God*. The testimony of the eyewitness requires no proof; but when we finally accept what really is the truth, then we will experience the peace and assurance that comes with knowing the truth.

The results of testimony

Whatever God does bears fruit. Since he's the one who is responsible for witnesses – since he's the reason we have them in the first place – we can be sure that he will achieve his purposes in sending out those witnesses. It may be for our good or for our destruction, but he *will* accomplish what he wants through them. For this reason alone, we ought to be wise and take notice whenever they speak to us. "We must pay more careful attention, therefore, to what we have heard ... how shall we escape if we ignore such a great salvation?" (Hebrews 2:1,3)

So, what does God accomplish by using witnesses? **First**, as we mentioned above, witnesses get us thinking about God for a change. We are so involved in living daily life that we forget about God, as if spiritual matters can be put off until the day we die. It can't, and those who think they can ignore spiritual issues until later will find that *there will be no time* to take care of them. For example, one man felt that he really must be about the business of increasing his wealth and making life more comfortable. Jesus called him a fool:

> You fool! This very night your life will be demanded from you. Then who will get what you have prepared for yourself? (Luke 12:20)

God *is* real, and anybody who convinces us of that truth is doing us a favor. Not only do we risk stumbling in the dark and falling into misery and emptiness without him, we miss out on tremendous spiritual blessings as well. There really is punishment for those who will not acknowledge their Creator, but there is blessing for those who turn to the Redeemer who cleanses from sin and makes us children of God. (Hebrews 11:6) Again, we would believe none of this if it weren't for those who have gone on before and discovered the reality of God. People have actually felt the wrath of God and died in terror of the God that they so carelessly offended. The rich man, for example, still testifies to us, through the story of Jesus, that it's folly to ignore God. (Luke 16:19-31) He wanted desperately to tell his brothers about that! Others have found that God is rich toward those who love him, that they have no unfilled needs, that they have found what their hearts desired. (Psalm 37:25) People nowadays often wonder if God really exists, because they don't see any proof that it makes a difference in one's life one way or another whether you believe in him or not. They need only to look in the Bible and they will see abundant testimony that he *is* real, and things *do* change for the better for his people. God is not someone's imagination; we simply can't account in any other way for what happens in people's lives – God's works are so miraculous and contrary to the way the world normally works that we can't ignore them.

Second, a witness teaches us important lessons. Living with God is a new experience, which none of us are ready for. How do we please him? What does he dislike? What does he want me to do with my life? How do I know that I am working with him and not against him? These and many other questions come naturally to mind when we find ourselves face to face with God who expects the impossible from an ignorant sinner! We must find answers, and reliable ones. "God is Spirit, and his worshippers must worship in Spirit and in truth." (John 4:24) It isn't obvious, this business of being a spiritually-aware and responsible citizen in the Kingdom of God. We have been too long trained in the physical world, and we need help to understand the new country that God has made us a part of.

The witness shows us how to have faith, how to obey the laws of God, what to put our trust in, how to relate to our enemies and friends, what is good and what is bad, how to live in the world and yet not be part of the world, how to carry the message of God's kingdom to the world, what to say and what not to say, how to glorify him and what to avoid because it dishonors him, and many other things. People all through the Bible discovered these truths through personal experience, and they knew that they were in God's presence when they learned them. The reason it was recorded in the Bible was so that we in our day might read it and meditate on it and learn from it.

Third, they are an encouragement for us. We need their testimony: what God expects of us is nothing less than a radical transformation. He expects us "to put off your old self, which is being corrupted by its deceitful desires; to be made new in the attitude of your minds; and to put on the new self, created to be like God in true righteousness and holiness." (Ephesians 4:22-24) Living with God is to be "born again." (John 3:3) We have to leave our sins behind, our old friends, our old ways, even many of the things of the world that we value the most. What we wonder, when faced with this drastic loss, is whether it's worth it! Those who have gone through the experience in the past, however, assure us that it *is* worth it. (Mark 10:29-30) Even when we have already been through it, it helps to go back to *their* testimony and re-read it as they encourage us to continue in what we have started.

We also need encouragement about what we've put our hope in. Even though we may have cast our lot with the Lord, we aren't going to get much of what he promises his children – not yet.

> All these people were still living by faith when they died. *They did not receive the things promised; they only saw them and welcomed them from a distance.* And they admitted that they were aliens and strangers on earth. People who say such things show that they are looking for a country of their own. If they had been thinking of the country they had left, they would have had opportunity to return. Instead, they were longing for a better country – a Heavenly one. Therefore God is not ashamed to be called their God, for he has prepared a city for them. (Hebrews 11:13-16)

We like to see evidence that we aren't putting our hopes on something that doesn't exist. We would like to know that there really is a Heaven, that there will be eternal life, that there will be justice, that God will get all the glory he deserves, that Jesus really is all that he says he is, that there really are treasures in Heaven for us. We do have hopes, and those hopes aren't empty daydreams but facts based on what others have discovered to be true. Our faith is "certain" and "sure" of things that our physical eyes can't see (Hebrews 11:1), because our spiritual eyes have been drawn to the realities of God's world by the testimony of those witnesses before us.

Fourth, there's also an unpleasant result of the testimony of God's witnesses. Remember that God's Word always does what he sends it out to do: "So is my Word that goes out from my mouth: it will not return to me empty, but will accomplish what I desire and achieve the purpose for which I sent it." (Isaiah 55:11) And sometimes he hardens hearts with it. There are those who hear the testimony of the saints and turn their backs on it; they want nothing to do with such a God. I know it sounds incredible, but God himself testifies that he is behind their hardness of heart:

> Go and tell this people: "Be ever hearing, but never understanding; be ever seeing, but never perceiving." Make the heart of this people calloused; make their ears dull and close their eyes. Otherwise they might see with their eyes, hear with their ears, understand with their hearts, and turn and be healed. (Isaiah 6:9-10)

And that's exactly what happens. Some people love their sin, they love this world, they love darkness, and they hate anything that has to do with God. They will not listen. When someone comes along and claims to have seen God and his work, and testifies to them about the reality of God, it makes their hearts hard against God and his people – so much so that they become "enemies of the cross of Christ." (Philippians 3:18) They deny, in the face of the evidence of reliable witnesses, the Sovereign Lord who bought them. (2 Peter 2:1) For example, Moses testified to Pharaoh about the Lord of Israel, and all it did was harden Pharaoh's heart against the Lord's command to release the Israelites. These people become determined enemies of the God they hear about.

But as the writer of Hebrews pointed out, "Even though we speak like this, dear friends, we are confident of better things in your case – things that accompany salvation." (Hebrews 6:9) The witnesses testify of the Word of Life, the power that sets us free from sin and death and lifts us up to the Heavenly realms. It would be a shame if this testimony of life would prove to be a curse on our heads. But it turns out one way or another, as Paul contemplated about his ministry: "To the one we are the smell of death; to the other, the fragrance of life." (2 Corinthians 2:16) Witnesses always have one effect or another with us.

False witnesses

Because the testimony of eyewitnesses is so important for deciding a case, it's a serious offense for a witness to give a false testimony. This is known as perjury, and there are heavy penalties for such crimes against the court. After all, someone's life, freedom and reputation depend on the testimony of witnesses. *It has to be true*.

In the Law of Moses we read about a sobering ceremony concerning witnesses who testify against the accused. If the accused man is found guilty, the witnesses who testified against him must be the first to lay hands on him: "The hands of the witnesses must be the first in putting him to death." (Deuteronomy 17:7) For this reason, the court will not accept false testimony, and if it has reason to think that a witness is lying then the entire case could be overturned along with punishing the false witness.

This is what God thinks about witnesses who give false testimony in his court:

There are six things the LORD hates, seven that are detestable to him ... a false witness who pours out lies. (Proverbs 6:16,19)

A truthful witness gives honest testimony, but a false witness tells lies. (Proverbs 12:17)

A truthful witness does not deceive, but a false witness pours out lies. (Proverbs 14:5)

A truthful witness saves lives, but a false witness is deceitful. (Proverbs 14:25)

A false witness will not go unpunished, and he who pours out lies will not go free. (Proverbs 19:5)

A false witness will not go unpunished, and he who pours out lies will perish. (Proverbs 19:9)

A corrupt witness mocks at justice, and the mouth of the wicked gulps down evil. (Proverbs 19:28)

A false witness will perish, and whoever listens to him will be destroyed forever. (Proverbs 21:28)

If this is what God thinks of false witnesses, you can be sure that he intends to select faithful witnesses when it comes to testifying about him. *The witnesses of God and his miracles gave the most trustworthy testimony ever given in the history of man.* This is the truth; it has to be, because every one of the witnesses of the Bible are under oath in God's court to tell the truth or be guilty of perjury against God himself. We can, therefore, rely completely on their testimony.

What do they witness about?

There are many things in God's kingdom that we just can't see on our own – either it's of a spiritual nature, or it seems impossible to us (and therefore couldn't possibly be true), or it's so new that we can't understand what we're looking at. This is to be expected: God's world isn't like ours, and he does things in ways that are new to us. "'For my thoughts are not your thoughts, neither are your ways my ways,' declares the LORD." (Isaiah 55:8) There are many things about us that get in the way of that clear view which we need to see God: our sin, our physical senses, the deceitfulness of the world and the devil, and even the fact that God hides himself from us.

But a salvation that we can't understand or take advantage of is of no use, is it? The mysteries of God have to become plain; they have to come within reach of our minds and hearts if they will do us any good. And this must be something that God does for us: he intends to make his spiritual treasures free and open to anybody who wants them. The problem to solve, however, is how to get the news to us about those treasures – in light of the tremendous obstacles that have always been in the way of that knowledge. So, he chose an effective way to make the truth plain and convincing to us: he sent eyewitnesses to us to clear up the mysteries.

> Although I am less than the least of all God's people, this grace was given me: to preach to the Gentiles the unsearchable riches of Christ, and to make plain to everyone the administration of this mystery, which for ages past was kept hidden in God, who created all things. (Ephesians 3:8-9)

So we will find the witnesses in the Bible testifying to *certain crucial truths* that God's people must learn about if they want to be saved. These are matters that deal with our salvation, with our consciences, with our eternal future, with our warfare against our enemy. They are not small or unimportant matters! Those who testified to the reality and nature of these things had a high calling; we all need this truth in order to live with God, yet nobody else knew the truth of these mysteries besides the eyewitnesses.

It's been the fashion in our century to doubt the witnesses of the Bible, as if those ancient people were naïve and didn't (or couldn't!) know the truth as we can know it with our modern sophistication. For example, it's rare to find a person who believes that the Bible itself is the very Word of God – in its entirety. They might be willing to admit that it contains, here and there, *some* of his words, but they don't want to believe that everything in it is from God's mouth. But if we don't see that, this raises some practical problems that result in serious spiritual defects:

First, nobody can agree then on what part is from God and what isn't! If the human writers created some of it apart from God's Spirit, how are we to tell which parts? Surely what they said would therefore have less authority than the parts that God himself spoke – but who's to tell which is authoritative and which isn't?

Second, that puts us in the position of judging the Word of God – deciding what is from God and what is the product of man's mind – and any generation that has tried that has only made a confusing mess of things.

Third, the sin in our hearts (either consciously or unconsciously) will steer us away from the very passages that give repentance, forgiveness and life. We don't want to hear about our sin, therefore we avoid those places that, like a surgeon's knife, want to identify it and cut it away. There will be no healing of the heart when the heart won't submit to the Lord's judgment of it.

Fourth, when we feel free to set a new standard for what is truth (that is, *our* opinions supported by a few choice passages from the Bible) then we really have no standard left – because everyone will feel free to make their own.

Fifth, and this is most critical and the thing that God will use to judge us, we are calling someone a liar when we don't accept the Bible as God's Word. It claims to be the Word of God, and we have no freedom to doubt that. God's honor is at stake when we doubt his Word in any way; we can expect to hear about this again on Judgment Day when God gets the glory he deserves.

So, doubting just one aspect of the reliability and source of information of the Bible – that is, the testimony of the witnesses – has tremendous and dangerous consequences for the life of the Church. If God's honor is important to us, and if we want to see sin and death defeated in the Church, we have to take the witnesses' testimony *at their word*. They claim no less an authority than God as the source for their information. We therefore have no freedom to doubt what they claim, and if we do doubt it we will lose everything.

As was mentioned before, the Bible's witnesses don't waste their time on unimportant issues. They testify about things that we are most ignorant of, the most deceived about – in fact, about those things that are most crucial for our spiritual well-being. These are matters that we can't find out about on our own. They touch the state of our souls, of our standing before God, of our fortunes on Judgment Day and beyond. If we listen to their message and act on it, we can redeem an entire lifetime that otherwise would have been wasted.

These are some of the important issues that the witnesses of the Bible deal with:

- **The Word of God** – Because we can't see God, because he hides himself in a cloud and in darkness, we really have no idea what he's like. Remember man's basic problem: we can't see or know God as he really is – because of our sin, our spiritual blindness, the veil that this world throws between us and him. And if we can't know God, what are people naturally going to do? They'll make up their own gods. They will dream up whatever they want their god to be and bow down to it. False religions all got their beginning from the ignorance of men driving them to create a god they could see and worship. But don't ask them to produce their god for us! They can't; so they make stories that explain why their god remains out of sight and is powerless to help them in time of need.

This is how the religions of the world all got their start: they made up a god that they have never seen, that they really don't know anything about. It's like the statue that the Athenians had on their hillside – "To the unknown God." (Acts 17:23) And since nobody has seen the true God, or heard his voice, none of their false gods matched what the Bible says the real God is like – they were really describing what they want *their* god to be like.

There have been a few people who did see God, however, and heard actual words that came from him. In his mercy, he broke his silence, drew near to earth, spoke to selected witnesses here and there, and charged them to convey his message to the rest of us. They heard his actual words! Now through them we will get to the truth about him – what he's really like, and what he actually thinks, without relying on the guesses of philosophers and religions.

The witnesses themselves knew that they heard God's voice; they knew that God gave them these words to pass on to others. And when they told others what they had heard, they were careful not to change the message in any way. There were penalties for that!

> I warn everyone who hears the words of the prophecy of this book: If anyone adds anything

to them, God will add to him the plagues described in this book. And if anyone takes words away from this book of prophecy, God will take away from him his share in the tree of life and in the holy city, which are described in this book. (Revelation 22:18-19)

There was no need for them to change the message they received from God. His own Word addresses the miserable condition of our souls in the best way possible. It gives life, when all other "truths" only prolongs our misery. His Word has power to change the soul, just as it reads, and lift it up into God's presence where we find treasures ready-made to relieve the damage that sin has done on our hearts. It gives faith, the will to obey his command, love for things of Heaven, hatred of God's enemies, courage to persevere. It's an accurate description of what Heaven is really like – and it describes our world, and our own souls, in clear pictures. Through it we can actually walk in the presence of God and experience the Spirit of God counseling us, guiding us, empowering us, and opening up our eyes to the reality of God. No, the human "authors" of the Bible didn't need to add or change anything to the Word that they were charged to pass on to us: it stands on its own and does its work without anybody's help.

The witnesses knew that what they spoke was directly from God, even when it appeared that they were finding their own words. For example, the Apostle Paul preached many times to many people, and what he said looks a lot like what modern preachers and teachers say in their lessons and sermons. But he knew that there was something different in his ministry, and he commended the Thessalonians for seeing the difference.

And we also thank God continually because, when you received the word of God, which you heard from us, you accepted it not as the word of men, *but as it actually is, the word of God*, which is at work in you who believe. (1 Thessalonians 2:13)

In fact, all of God's witnesses carried the same urgency in their messages because of the real source of their words. They can press the authority of God on our consciences, so much so that, when we read this "ancient" book, we cringe under its judgment of our sinful hearts. They knew that God was speaking through them to us. Peter tells us that ...

> Above all, you must understand that no prophecy of Scripture came about by the prophet's own interpretation. For prophecy never had its origin in the will of man, but men spoke from God as they were carried along by the Holy Spirit. (2 Peter 1:20-21)

This is a very plain statement about the origin of the message of a witness. It's not from the person himself; we can't afford to make that mistake about it. It transcends any single man – or even culture. It addresses the universal state of man; it speaks to the heart of men, women and children all over the world, from every culture, in all times and seasons. It's a textbook of faith and religious practice for every human creature that God made.

All other sources of religious truth are only true as they get their information from the Bible. Since the witnesses of God are the only ones who can claim to have seen God – and since their testimony is recorded only in the history of Israel and the Christian Church – that means the Bible is our sole authority, our only source of information about God that is absolutely reliable. Other authors may borrow from it, may analyze it – but they can be judged by it too. They are right in whatever they say about God only so far as they stick to the Bible's clear account of him; anything that they say about God that differs from the Bible is *wrong*.

The Bible describes a God who is different from us. His ways aren't like our ways: his works come out of Heaven, ours from the created earth; he approaches things as the Creator, we as the creatures. He works miracles – going around natural processes to accomplish his will – and we work through science and "cause and effect." Certainly we would expect that when this God speaks to us, not only will his ideas sound strange and unlikely to us, but it will be obvious that this isn't the product of men's minds. We don't think and work this way!

There is, however, a problem. Lies abound in our world. And since God's great enemy, Satan, has made it his "career" to smear God's character with lies, we should expect to run into all sorts of explanations about what God is like that just aren't true. They don't agree with the Bible's account of him, and they don't make any pretense about trying to agree with it. There are too many liars willing to teach it, and too many sinners ready to hear it! What about those who claim to be witnesses of God but aren't? Many times in war the enemy will send his men among us disguised as one of us, causing tremendous confusion, trying to lead us astray. Satan has his messengers too, and he makes them as appealing as possible in order to deceive us. They are well-trained, ruthless, deceitful, and smooth-talking. What they say about God, even though it contradicts the Bible, sounds so reasonable. Their aim, however, is to get us away from the Bible and believe *anything* else than the truth.

> For Satan himself masquerades as an angel of light. It is not surprising, then, if his servants masquerade as servants of

righteousness. Their end will be what their actions deserve. (2 Corinthians 11:14-15)

As you know, traitors are shot in times of war. Those who claim to bear the message of God, but who really were not sent by God and never heard any such thing from God, will find that they have a terrible judgment to look forward to. "Not many of you should presume to be teachers, my brothers, because you know that we who teach will be judged more strictly." (James 3:1)

If a prophet, or one who foretells by dreams, appears among you and announces to you a miraculous sign or wonder, and if the sign or wonder of which he has spoken takes place, and he says, "Let us follow other gods" (gods you have not known) "and let us worship them," you must not listen to the words of that prophet or dreamer. The LORD your God is testing you to find out whether you love him with all your heart and with all your soul. (Deuteronomy 13:1-3)

The reason that the judgment is so severe against a false prophet is that our spiritual well-being depends on his words; they must be from God (and therefore life-giving) to do us any good. Any other source would be like poison to us. The Lord will not tolerate false witnesses who poison his people with lies.

- **Creation** – Probably the most important event that has ever happened in the history of the universe, besides the life of Christ, was Creation. This is where everything began: the stars, the earth, life, mankind. Even unbelievers know how important it is to know *how* the universe came to be, because that will provide a lot of answers to other pressing questions. For example, if the universe was just a chaotic jumble that turned out to be what it is today through chance, then there is no special design or purpose behind it, and there is no particular goal that it's aiming for. But if God made it, then it works according to his master plan and is gradually carrying us all to the Last Day, when the plan will be finished. So, we need to know what really happened at the beginning.

According to most scientists, the world is no more than matter and energy that has always existed. Evolutionary processes mixed the two together and produced a universe. Blind chance, in other words, along with the principles of physics and chemistry, made the world. And how do they know this? Through sheer conjecture! Nobody was there at the beginning, so they rely on mathematics and the uniformitarian principle (the idea that the world has always existed under the same forces moving at the same rate as what we see in our present day) to reason backwards billions of years to a "beginning." Science also relies on physical "evidence" that supposedly tells its own story of the beginning.

And on the Bible's side? There *is* an account of how the world started in Genesis, but unfortunately there were no human witnesses! Man wasn't created until the sixth day and, naturally, couldn't have seen what happened *before* he showed up on the scene. Not only that, the Bible's account is contrary to scientific principles – in fact, it contradicts common sense and reason. According to the story, the world was made through miracles – in days – which every modern man knows couldn't have happened. And the Bible describes a spiritual God making the world, which again modern science knows nothing about and can't see with its instruments.

Now, since hardly anybody believes that Creation happened in six days as Genesis 1 claims, there are many arguments about how, reasonably speaking, the world could have evolved to its present form. And since there are no witnesses, who is to say that science is wrong about this?

The problem is this: if science is right, then there was little or nothing for God to do in making the world; it sort of fell together on its own. That means that there is no purpose to things, that man isn't a special creation, that he is only the capstone of the animal kingdom and made up of the same basic parts. And that leads to no soul, no morality, and no hope of Heaven – in fact, absolutely no need for God himself. As you can see, there is too much at stake here to let this problem go unsolved.

If you know anything about how God works, you would know that God doesn't leave himself without witnesses when he works on earth, because he knows we will doubt his bare word of what happened unless someone can step up and claim that he *saw* God do it. And for Creation, the witness is the Holy Spirit:

> In the beginning God created the heavens and the earth. Now the earth was formless and empty, darkness was over the surface of the deep, *and the Spirit of God was hovering over the waters.* (Genesis 1:1-2)

As we shall see later, the Spirit is the expert witness of the works of God. He knows the mind of God, he understands the works of God, he knows the plans of God, he testifies in order to glorify God in all things. We can absolutely rely on whatever the Spirit tells us about God. The Spirit is a more reliable witness than any other person we could turn to. It's fortunate for us, then, that we have *this* witness of Creation, because otherwise we might have reason to believe that the author of this account in Genesis must have gotten it wrong. The account seems too impossible to believe! It certainly doesn't square with common sense. But we cannot doubt the integrity of the witness in this case; since the witness is the Spirit of God, it would be the same as doubting whether God can explain what he himself did!

Remember that Moses wrote Genesis, and the Bible calls him the greatest of the Prophets. (Deuteronomy 34:10) And Peter, as we have seen, assures us that no prophet spoke his own words, but only what the Spirit of God moved him to say. In the story of Creation, therefore, the only witness of this event carefully described it to Moses who wrote it down for us. So, what should be our conclusion about the Genesis account? *That this is the only correct way of describing what happened.* A scientific description of the world's beginning doesn't do it justice – doesn't even come close to it. There were huge spiritual realities at work there that can't be seen or known through the physical senses. The Bible is the window into a bigger world than a natural approach can show us. And therefore, through the Bible we will be able to see where we fit into this bigger picture of a spiritual-physical creation.

Genesis isn't the only place where Creation is explained to us. For example, we learn that God created the world in wisdom and understanding:

> By wisdom the LORD laid the earth's foundations, by understanding he set the heavens in place; by his knowledge the deeps were divided, and the clouds let drop the dew. (Proverbs 3:19-20)

Not only does this account for the amazing way the world works with efficiency and harmony, it gives us an insight into the Lord's deeper purposes. Everything in the universe is going to bring him glory; he designed it to do this. The world is a stage, a setting for the great works of redemption and the springboard for the new spiritual kingdom that he had in mind from the beginning. The physical world serves a greater purpose than simply providing us with food and drink and work! In God's amazing wisdom, it led to the Church and the work of Christ on the cross – and it will eventually lead us all to Judgment Day.

There are other things about Creation that we learn from the witnesses in the Bible. For example, God made the world through Christ, he commanded things into existence, he made it for his glory, he set it on firm foundations, and he created man to rule over the new earth. These other "Creation passages" explain the realities behind a lot of what makes up our lives, in ways that science can't hope to explain for us. They are invaluable windows into the past that show us what God really did. Knowing these things, we can get a better idea of what we need to be doing now if we want to work *with* God, instead of against him, in his Creation.

- **Miracles** – In our day, since science reigns supreme in the public eye, it is intellectual suicide to believe in miracles. We use the word all the time – like "miracle of medicine" or "it's a miracle that it happened!" – but we really don't mean what the Bible means by it. We are taught that those ancient people just didn't understand natural phenomena as we do – that's why they called anything they couldn't explain a miracle.

But we can't play with the Bible like that. Knowing full well that there would be skeptics like us who would doubt that such things could have happened, God made sure that there was a witness present to testify to the truth. For example, even with our modern sophistication, we stand amazed at the story about Jesus walking on water. There is no explaining that miracle in terms understandable to the human mind. And the disciples saw him do it; that's what clinches the story. We can doubt it if we like, but with so many people who were there and who testified to the event, we either must believe it or call the whole boatload of them liars!

Miracles are an integral part of the Bible's story. Why would God resort to using miracles in the first place? Because the world simply can't give us what our souls need. We are caught in blind natural forces that are bigger than we are, and we inevitably lose to the crush of those forces. We are helpless before sin and death. For a while we can struggle on under life's problems on our own strength, but death inevitably catches up with all of us and we will lose the fight. We are caught in the trap of wickedness and rebellion (born in our own hearts, where we have the least will and strength to resist it!), frustrations, sickness, enemies, circumstances – we can't change things, nor can we escape the sentence of death against us. We need someone who is above the world, who isn't constrained by the limitations of time and space. We need someone who can do the impossible.

God does the impossible – because we need it. He brings resources and power from Heaven to bear on our problems. He fixes what is broken on earth. He puts a crumbling physical reality on a solid spiritual foundation. And with these miracles he's building a new kind of world that will eventually replace the present one.

And when we see him so easily solve our problems through miracles, we take confidence in him and start leaning on his arm instead of our own strength. We take our stand in his spiritual world and turn our backs on the fallen first Creation. There are many good reasons, therefore, for God to use miracles!

So, miracles are still an extremely important aspect of God's growing Kingdom. And if he still uses miracles – if they are the foundation of his work from the beginning – we need to know for certain whether the miracles of the Bible really happened. And fortunately we do have witnesses for all these miracles. They were there; they saw God do these amazing things. And they testify to us that we have a God who does the impossible. Now, does that have anything to do with our prayers? Our worship? Our faith in him? It should! We ought to pay attention to what these witnesses tell us about what God can do for his people, because *he will do the same for us*. As Habakkuk the prophet prayed, so should we:

> LORD, I have heard of your fame; I stand in awe of your deeds, O LORD. Renew them in our day, in our time make them known; in wrath remember mercy. (Habakkuk 3:2)

- **The Coming Kingdom** – Though the world we live in is God's creation – and we know that he loves the world he made (see John 3:16) – there is another "world" that God hates passionately. It's what John refers to when he warns us:

> Do not love the world or anything in the world. If anyone loves the world, the love of the Father is not in him. For everything in the world – the cravings of sinful man, the lust of his eyes and the boasting of what he has and does – comes not from the Father but from the world. (1 John 2:15-16)

It's a kingdom of darkness, and the devil rules over it to lead us all into ignorance and death and destruction. We are all a part of it from birth. It's a kingdom of lies. We are all born ignorant of God, and even of ourselves and the world that we're a part of. We make advances and progress in the world and then get set back – through war, famine, sickness, frustration, and suffering. We make the world we want, and use our new-found powers of science to do it

– and still suffer and die in the end for all the effort we throw into it. Death rules in this world. Our crime? We have created the world that *we* want instead of accepted the world that God created for us. In the world of our making we think that we are free to sin, and we try to fight off the curse of death – but we can't win, because God hates the world of wickedness and rebellion that we've built for ourselves.

> As for you, you were dead in your transgressions and sins, in which you used to live when you followed the ways of this world and of the ruler of the kingdom of the air, the spirit who is now at work in those who are disobedient. All of us also lived among them at one time, gratifying the cravings of our sinful nature and following its desires and thoughts. Like the rest, we were by nature objects of wrath. (Ephesians 2:1-3)

How would you feel if a stranger came to your home and told you that a terrifying and ruthless enemy was on his way with a powerful army to destroy you and your community? What if he told you that there was no escape, that the enemy was looking for rebels and that you will surely die, that there is nothing that you can do to protect yourself – unless you surrender *now*? Would it make you change your ways? Would you try to find a way out of the coming disaster? You would probably get busy finding out how you could switch sides!

The Bible tells us this very thing – it says that God's army is coming and he intends to destroy this world, the kingdom of darkness and its ruler and all of its rebellious subjects. He won't continue to put up with the misery and destruction that we have inflicted on his creation; he intends to come and tear it all down and build "a new heavens and a new earth." (Isaiah 65:17)

Though God has fairly warned us, we hear about this news and yet we don't take it very seriously. Life goes on, sin goes unpunished, and he hasn't done anything yet! "When the sentence for a crime is not quickly carried out, the hearts of the people are filled with schemes to do wrong." (Ecclesiastes 8:11)

> Where is this 'coming' he promised? Ever since our fathers died, everything goes on as it has since the beginning of creation. (2 Peter 3:4)

So God raised up witnesses: there are those who have seen the army of God setting out from the gates of Heaven, and it's heading this way.

> I saw Heaven standing open and there before me was a white horse, whose rider is called Faithful and True. With justice he judges and makes war. His eyes are like blazing fire, and on his head are many crowns. He has a name written on him that no one knows but he himself. He is dressed in a robe dipped in blood, and his name is the Word of God. The armies of heaven were following him, riding on white horses and dressed in fine linen, white and clean. Out of his mouth comes a sharp sword with which to strike down the nations. "He will rule them with an iron scepter." He treads the winepress of the fury of the wrath of God Almighty. On his robe and on his thigh he has this name written: KING OF KINGS AND LORD OF LORDS. (Revelation 19:11-16)

You see, it wasn't just an idle threat. God really is coming; John saw him. There's only a short time left for this world, and sinners need to take the testimony of witnesses seriously and repent *now*, before it's too late. If the Son of Man comes and catches them in their sin, still in the service of the lord of darkness, fighting under the banner of wickedness, *there will be no mercy shown.* Only if they throw down their swords now and believe the Gospel of the Kingdom will they find mercy from the King of kings. It would be foolish to continue in your sins when there are those who have seen the King coming to destroy sinners.

What will the new Kingdom of God be like? We also have eyewitness testimony for that. The Bible's witnesses have seen the new world that God has in mind for his subjects. They have also seen what God intends to do to his people themselves – he plans to remake them and make them fit for living in an eternal, spiritual, holy Kingdom. It will be a new world with new creatures doing a new kind of work for the glory of God. There won't be any traces of the old world left in it. So, anybody looking forward to a change from this world and the way it works will find the testimony of these witnesses to be "good news."

- **Jesus Christ** – It says in Philippians that Christ set aside his glory before coming into this world. It was necessary for him to do that, but it has caused so much confusion in the minds of people throughout history that unless we have some help, we will miss entirely what he is all about.

His outward circumstances give us no clue at all as to his real nature. He was born to poor parents, learned carpentry, and had no formal education and no opportunity for advancement in society. When he began his public ministry, he spent his time on the road – he had no place to lay his head, and could offer no physical rewards to his followers. He made enemies with the political and religious leaders. He purposely avoided doing showy things to get attention or a popular following. Everything he did and said was misunderstood by somebody, somewhere; even his own disciples often missed the point. Finally he was shamed and put to death by his own people, and forgotten. The Jews went on with their lives as if he had never lived among them.

That's not a very promising start for the King of God's Kingdom! If history is to have a more favorable judgment of this man, we need more information about who he was. And we especially aren't going to learn any more about him if we rely on the Jews' account of him! Fortunately we do have a better source of information – the testimony of witnesses *who saw the true Jesus*. They saw the deeper reality in Jesus that everyone else missed. Through their eyes we can learn where Jesus came from, what he did, where he went from here, and what he's doing this very minute.

The Old Testament Prophets saw who he was and foretold his coming. They told us that he was the Son of David, coming to sit on David's throne and rule God's people forever in justice and righteousness. They told us that he is the eternal sacrifice that would take away the sins of his people forever. They told us that his Kingdom is spiritual and will transform the heart of each believer. In fact, they left little to wonder about, since they described the King and his work so carefully. How did they know all this about Jesus? How could they be sure of his true nature? They saw it – God showed it to them. "Your father Abraham rejoiced at the thought of seeing my day; *he saw it* and was glad." (John 8:56) God's eyewitnesses don't lie; they tell us what they saw, and our only option is to believe them – especially since we won't get a chance to see what they saw.

The disciples saw, gradually, who Jesus was, and their subsequent ministries were devoted to spreading the testimony of the Christ. Paul called the story of Jesus a mystery: there is nothing about this perplexing man that would cause us, at first glance, to depend on him for anything. But after reading the testimony of the Apostles, we gain a new appreciation and wonder for Jesus Christ. He literally is our life, our only hope, our God in the flesh within our reach.

The Church also testifies about Christ in the preaching of the Gospel and life among the saints. Preaching and teaching makes people interested to hear more; the testimonies, if true, hold rich promise for those who are weary of this world. And when people see the children of God living in peace, loving each other, skillfully destroying the works of the devil and building an eternal kingdom – well, such things are proof of the power of Christ among his people; they couldn't happen otherwise.

We also have testimony from those who know what Jesus is doing now for his people. They saw him in Heaven interceding for them, getting spiritual resources in answer to their prayers, and sending those treasures to them through the Spirit. They know how a person can get in touch with Jesus. They also know what will happen to those who ignore Jesus: he's a King, and he's coming to carry out justice on the earth. He's a lifesaver offered freely by God to those who are dying and doomed. Finally, these witnesses tell us how we can know when Jesus is present and working in a church: he takes personal charge of things, and lives among them, and insists that we make room for him and trust him to do his part in the life of the church. There are ways to work with him, and penalties for working against him or trying to do his work for him. The witnesses teach us about all these things.

There will always be witnesses for Christ – there *must* be witnesses – because God's will for this world is that men and women hear the Gospel, believe in Christ, and be saved. Sometimes we fear that the Church will be overcome by her enemies, or that her internal fights will destroy her. But God will always have witnesses who can testify that Jesus still lives and answers prayer, and saves his people from the power of sin. God put his whole being into Jesus (Colossians 1:19), so he is determined to focus our attention on him.

- **New Life** – One of the most powerful testimonies of the reality of God and the redemption that is in Christ is a changed life. When someone suddenly, unexplainably, changes from a hardened sinner into a humble and righteous saint, there is something going on here that can't be explained easily. It's hard to argue against undeniable results.

By now, so many people have heard the story of Jesus so many times that they almost have it memorized. Yet it makes almost no impression on most people. It's like the story of Buddha or Mohammed – an ancient tale from long ago, but of no use for us now. We know that the Bible says that God will create a new heart in us (Ezekiel 36:26), that we must be born again (John 3:3), that our citizenship will be in Heaven (Philippians 3:20) – but it sounds more like a fairy tale than fact. Why *should* anybody take it seriously when it's just one philosophy among the world's many?

So you can imagine the surprise of most people when someone stands up and claims to have met Jesus personally. He tells us that, because of Christ, he has experienced a spiritual rebirth, and he can see and hear things now that he couldn't before. He knows that something happened in his heart, because the old desire for sin is strangely quiet now and has been replaced by a desire to please God in everything. We look at this man, wondering what he has experienced, and find ourselves wishing that we could experience the same thing.

A witness to the new life in Christ has some surprises for us! His message isn't at all what we were expecting about what Christianity would be. He tells us how to become a Christian – which isn't the way most people would have thought to go about it. He tells us why we need to be saved and become one with Christ, which doesn't sit well with our pride, nor were we aware of the danger we are in until we do. He tells us the results of being a Christian which, again, surprise us, because we were hoping that God would do different things than these which we hear about. But looking at this witness, who has undergone a complete life-change and seemingly for the better, how can we argue with the results? If we want to be healed in the same way, then we have to accept his testimony and come to the Lord too.

It's this kind of testimony that makes the Kingdom of God grow from age to age. New converts are constantly entering the ranks of God's people because they heard the testimony of those who have seen Jesus by faith. There's no hard proof that such a thing happens to someone; we can't measure anything about them with instruments, or prove it with logic. But it's real nonetheless, and difficult to argue with. Even hardened sinners are impressed with how real God must be to Christians, even though they may have no intention of trying it themselves!

> Live such good lives among the pagans that, though they accuse you of doing wrong, they may see your good deeds and glorify God on the day he visits us. (1 Peter 2:12)

- **The Nature of the world** – Though we are all in love with the world, and hate the idea of having to give it up, there is some bad news from God's witnesses:

> By the same word the present heavens and earth are reserved for fire, being kept for the day

of judgment and destruction of ungodly men. (2 Peter 3:7)

God has always planned to do away with this physical world, ever since the beginning. If Adam and Eve wouldn't have sinned, the world probably would have gone on forever – or at least for a long time, because it served God's purposes as a perfect home for humans. But sin changed the situation. The world is being corrupted by the wickedness of men and women. It isn't the same perfect world that God first created.

In the beginning, when God made the world, he looked at it and saw that it was "very good." (Genesis 1:31) Even man was perfect: "God made mankind upright." (Ecclesiastes 7:29) The idea here is that the world didn't need anything more done to it to make it perfect. Any changes would have taken away from its perfection, not added to it. We have the Spirit's testimony to that perfection of Creation, since he was there when God made the world.

When man sinned and rebelled against God's authority, the situation changed completely. "God made mankind upright, but men have gone in search of many schemes." (Ecclesiastes 7:29) In other words, the world as God made it wasn't good enough for sinful man. In order to accommodate his inclinations to self-pleasure, self-rule, and self-worship, the world had to be remade to fit in with his new plans. So, his "improvements" have only ruined the world for the most part. If you think about it, there seems to be a corresponding evil result to every so-called advancement in our society. For example, the radio and TV, though innocent and powerful tools in themselves, have made it possible for the forces of darkness to take hold of and rule the minds of billions all around the world. The automobile, though giving us tremendous possibilities for transport and travel, has been instrumental in breaking up the community and family as everyone has "hit the road" and moved away to far places. Public schools, though a good idea in themselves, have become breeding grounds for raising criminals, rebels, and unbelievers. The examples are endless. There seems to be a "dark side" to almost every improvement that we make to our lives.

When we build up a world of our own that we are pleased with – we make rules to govern ourselves by, and we fill our hours and homes with its pleasures – we have actually remade the world into a new "creation" in our own image. Our own world suits us better than what God wants for us. This is the "world" that John warns us against:

> Do not love the world or anything in the world. If anyone loves the world, the love of the Father is not in him. For everything in the world – the cravings of sinful man, the lust of his eyes and the boasting of what he has and does – comes not from the Father but from the world. The world and its desires pass away, but the man who does the will of God lives forever. (1 John 2:15-17)

This world, we are told in Ecclesiastes, is empty – we're fooling ourselves if we think we will get the pleasure and fulfillment out of it that we work so hard for:

> "Meaningless! Meaningless!" says the Teacher. "Utterly meaningless! Everything is meaningless." What does man gain from all his labor at which he toils under the sun? Generations come and generations go, but the earth remains forever. The sun rises and the sun sets, and hurries back to where it rises. The wind blows to the south and turns to the north; round and round it goes, ever returning on its course. All streams flow into the sea,

yet the sea is never full. To the place the streams come from, there they return again. All things are wearisome, more than one can say. The eye never has enough of seeing, nor the ear its fill of hearing. What has been will be again, what has been done will be done again; there is nothing new under the sun. Is there anything of which one can say, "Look! This is something new"? It was here already, long ago; it was here before our time. There is no remembrance of men of old, and even those who are yet to come will not be remembered by those who follow. (Ecclesiastes 1:1-11)

Solomon searched this matter out, he claimed, and the Lord showed him what the world was really like. He certainly had the opportunity of discovering the meaning of whatever the world had in store for him! But after all that searching, he found it empty and meaningless. His testimony, therefore, should set us thinking about the world we live in: we won't find any more meaning in our world than he did in his.

What is the world, then, in God's hands? It's a stage upon which we are playing out our roles before God. He put us in this world, took away our ability to see the spiritual forces surrounding us, gave us his Law, and commands us to fear and obey him. Will we? Will we waste our lives and strength on things that don't matter, on this world's riches that will one day be destroyed? Or will we believe the testimony of the Bible's witnesses warning us against working for what is doomed to be destroyed? Will we instead put our hearts and minds on "things above, where Christ is seated at the right hand of God?" (Colossians 3:1) And on Judgment Day God will review what we've done with our lives (after he has destroyed the world, which will then be of no more use to him):

> For we must all appear before the judgment seat of Christ, that each one may receive what is due him for the things done while in the body, whether good or bad. (2 Corinthians 5:10)

That's why Jesus counseled us to "store up for yourselves treasures in Heaven" (Matthew 6:20) – the "treasures" of this world aren't worth the effort. That's why the writer of Proverbs counseled us to get wisdom, which is worth more than fine gold and silver. (Proverbs 8:19) And that's why the saints of Bible times scorned the riches of this world and instead looked forward to a better world –

> He regarded disgrace for the sake of Christ as of greater value than the treasures of Egypt, because he was looking ahead to his reward. (Hebrews 11:26)

These people have seen the nature of our world and have turned their backs on it. They of course found it easy to do that, because they also saw the world that God has planned for his people – it's far better than anything we have here. The other thing that they saw was that one can't hold on to the promises of both worlds: God calls us to *forsake* this world and put our hope on his spiritual world. Jesus knew what is in the heart of man, that he can't be loyal to two opposing world systems:

> No one can serve two masters. Either he will hate the one and love the other, or he will be devoted to the one and despise the other. You cannot serve both God and Money. (Matthew 6:24)

That too is an insight into the nature of the treasures of this physical world: they blind the soul to the reality of God; they lure us away from the riches of

Heaven; they are dangerous enemies to our spiritual state. One accumulates them to one's ruin, like drinking poison. We may think that we can safely accumulate and enjoy our physical prosperity and pleasures, but these things gradually deaden us to the voice of God in the Bible calling us to God's spiritual treasures instead. A rich man has little time for the things of God, the witnesses of God tell us:

> The brother in humble circumstances ought to take pride in his high position. But the one who is rich should take pride in his low position, because he will pass away like a wild flower. For the sun rises with scorching heat and withers the plant; its blossom falls and its beauty is destroyed. In the same way, the rich man will fade away even while he goes about his business. (James 1:9-11)

- **Judgment Day** – Every human being knows what justice is. When someone doesn't get what he deserves, we get upset about that and complain that "something ought to be done about it." When courts let lawbreakers go free, only the wicked rejoice; the righteous are angry that justice wasn't done.

But before we can have justice, we first have to find out the facts. In a court of law, the judge is appointed to gather all the facts of the case and then give his judgment. We've already looked at this procedure. He can and should use the testimony of eyewitnesses, as well as any available evidence, to form his judgment.

God also will have his day in court. He is planning a great day of Judgment when he will bring every human being, dead or alive, before his throne to be examined:

What do they witness about? – 73

> Then I saw a great white throne and him who was seated on it. Earth and sky fled from his presence, and there was no place for them. And I saw the dead, great and small, standing before the throne, and books were opened. Another book was opened, which is the book of life. The dead were judged according to what they had done as recorded in the books. The sea gave up the dead that were in it, and death and Hades gave up the dead that were in them, and each person was judged according to what he had done. (Revelation 20:11-13)

This day is extremely important to God. We have to go back to Creation to understand why Judgment Day is so necessary. There, we saw, he made the world to his own specifications; it was all "very good" because it was ready and able to carry out his will for it. The world was designed to glorify God, primarily, and serve as a platform for man's activities as ruler over God's Kingdom.

Even though sin ruined the original Kingdom, God never lost control of the situation. He just changed the strategy. Now, instead of the original pristine, perfect Kingdom in which man would carry out God's orders, God starts recording the wrongs, the ruination, the failures and destruction of a ruler gone mad. What we have done in God's creation is imprinted into it with more permanence and damning evidence than words carved in stone. Like an eternal book, the ruined world that we "rule" over will be a testimony against us on Judgment Day.

As you can see, God is keen on bringing the criminal to justice. You can imagine what he feels like when he watches us ruin his Creation and rebel against his just Law. He is looking forward to the Day when he will put everything right again and punish the Lawbreakers.

For if God did not spare angels when they sinned, but sent them to hell, putting them into gloomy dungeons to be held for judgment; if he did not spare the ancient world when he brought the flood on its ungodly people, but protected Noah, a preacher of righteousness, and seven others; if he condemned the cities of Sodom and Gomorrah by burning them to ashes, and made them an example of what is going to happen to the ungodly; and if he rescued Lot, a righteous man, who was distressed by the filthy lives of lawless men (for that righteous man, living among them day after day, was tormented in his righteous soul by the lawless deeds he saw and heard) – if this is so, then the Lord knows how to rescue godly men from trials and to hold the unrighteous for the day of judgment, while continuing their punishment. This is especially true of those who follow the corrupt desire of the sinful nature and despise authority. (2 Peter 2:4-10)

We mustn't forget the righteous, though. God also has plans for them. They honored him as their Creator, depended on his goodness, turned to him for forgiveness for the sins they had committed against him, turned their backs on the world and set their hopes on Heaven, and devoted their entire lives to God's service and glory. God's reward for them will be greater service, more of Jesus whom they love, Heaven's treasures, total moral perfection, and no trace of the old life of sin and death that they had to struggle through in this world. Isaiah saw that new life and gives us his eyewitness account:

Behold, I will create new heavens and a new earth. The former things will not be remembered, nor will they come to mind. But be glad and rejoice forever in what I will create, for I will create Jerusalem to be a delight and its people a joy. I will rejoice over Jerusalem and take delight in my people; the sound of weeping and of crying will be heard in it no more ... The wolf and the lamb will feed together, and the lion will eat straw like the ox, but dust will be the serpent's food. They will neither harm nor destroy on all my holy mountain," says the LORD. (Isaiah 66:17-19, 25)

Heaven and Hell are fitting rewards for the righteous and wicked. Hell is the more problematic of the two, because we can't imagine God being so vicious as to condemn anybody, no matter how wicked they are, to eternal misery. But witnesses assure us that God's justice here is flawless. They have seen what the wicked are really like:

They are clouds without rain, blown along by the wind; autumn trees, without fruit and uprooted – twice dead. They are wild waves of the sea, foaming up their shame; wandering stars, for whom blackest darkness has been reserved forever. (Jude 12-13)

For although they knew God, they neither glorified him as God nor gave thanks to him, but their thinking became futile and their foolish hearts were darkened. Although they claimed to be wise, they became fools. (Romans 1:21-22)

There is no one righteous, not even one; there is no one who understands, no one who seeks God. (Romans 3:10-11)

These are accurate descriptions of the human heart in rebellion against God. They deserve nothing good from him. They don't want anything from God. Though the prospect of eternal misery would be terrifying to them, they asked for it: they also *don't want* to be with God forever! They will find out that God is harsher than they gave him credit for. He's a "hard man" who expects a spiritual profit. He won't hesitate to "fire" us when we don't do as he commands!

The righteous, however, will discover Heaven to be a fitting reward for their faith and labors. They will find that God had been giving them foretastes of Heaven all along, through the Spirit, giving them strength and hope to continue under the burdens of life. They will see in Heaven the reality behind the promises and helps that God gave them in this world. So it won't be an unfamiliar place to them; instead it will be the fullness of what they had been hoping for and enjoying all along – in fact, it will be exactly what they read about in the testimonies of the Bible's eyewitnesses.

The Witness of the Spirit

When it comes to a witness, there is no more reliable one than the Holy Spirit. We little appreciate what a tremendously valuable source of inside information that we have here. The Spirit can show us things that nobody else has the ability to show us – even the very thoughts that are going through God's mind. And we know for certain, when the Spirit shows us something, that we are getting the truth – he is called the "Spirit of truth." (John 14:17)

So the Spirit is essential for any kind of witnessing. He is unique because of his position; that is, since he himself is God, he speaks what he knows because *he's* the subject of the testimony. You can't get any more reliable testimony about the things of God than from God himself! The Spirit plays an essential role in God's kingdom in that he, being God, reveals the hidden things of God to us in a way that we can understand them.

> The Spirit searches all things, even the deep things of God. For who among men knows the thoughts of a man except the man's spirit within him? In the same way no one knows the thoughts of God except the Spirit of God. We have not received the spirit of the world but the Spirit who is from God, that we may understand what God has freely given us. This is what we speak, not in words taught us by human wisdom but in words taught by the Spirit, expressing spiritual truths in spiritual words. (1 Corinthians 2:10-13)

This is as close to the source as you can get. We not only see who we are dealing with here (the Spirit is God himself), but why we need his testimony: because God is *spiritual*, and the human mind can't naturally grasp such a reality without help. Plus, the things that God has in mind to give his people are not of this world. Riches, pleasures, jobs, homes, friends, all these things are easy to understand because they are part of our physical world. But God has higher things in mind, treasures in Heaven (Matthew 6:20-21), which to the unspiritual mind make no sense at all. To those whom the Spirit has taught, however, they become more precious than anything this world has to offer. God is spiritual, he's the Creator who made all things a certain way, he's the Judge and standard of Law by which we will be judged, he's the Redeemer who knows how to save us and what to save us from, he's the King and Lord who rules over all the world and achieves his purposes. In order to fully grasp this God, and know how to relate to this God, we need expert help.

The two functions of the Spirit

Usually we think of the Spirit in terms of sanctification – that is, making us free from sin, or holy. "But you were washed, you were *sanctified*, you were justified in the name of the Lord Jesus Christ and by the Spirit of our God." (1 Corinthians 6:11) "To God's elect … who have been chosen according to the foreknowledge of God the Father, by the *sanctifying* work of the Spirit, for obedience to Jesus Christ and sprinkling by his blood." (1 Peter 1:1-2)

But that's not the *primary* work of the Spirit according to the Bible. In a total of over 80 different passages that talk about what the Spirit does, I found only five places where it refers to his work of cleansing from sin, and some of those are marginal. Over half of the passages teach that the Spirit *reveals* the things of God, and the other half talk about the Spirit's *empowering* work.

- ***The Spirit reveals the world of God.*** " 'No eye has seen, no ear has heard, no mind has conceived what God has prepared for those who love him' – but God has revealed it to us by his Spirit." (1 Corinthians 2:9-10)

If we want to know more about Heaven, the first hurdle that we have to get over is the fact that we are so earthbound. Since the day we were born, we have known only what we can see, smell, touch, taste, and hear. This world that we live in has been, to us, the only real world, as far as we can tell. The things that we put value on and the things that we own are in this world; the issues that we consider important are in this world; the people we respect are in this world; the forces that we fear are in this world. Most people live and die knowing nothing more than what is in this physical world, and they really don't care if there is another world – it seems like unrealistic stories anyway, myths and fairy tales.

But there *is* another world that is different than this one, even if we don't know anything about it: it's the world that God lives in. God is not of this world. That's a fundamental doctrine of Christianity; we have to believe that God's world is a completely different place than this world that we live in, that he can and does exist without any dependence on the physical world. He's the Creator: he made the universe, and he doesn't depend on it in the least – it depends on him. We could all snap completely out of existence and he wouldn't change in the least. He is what he is, and he will always be what he is, without our help or interference.

God's world is completely different from ours. Whereas ours is always changing, always deteriorating and building up, his is unchanging. Ours is completely physical, which means that the One who made it can unmake it just as easily (which he intends to do someday, by the way); but God's world is spiritual and therefore eternal. Our world looks good on the outside, and promises to satisfy us – but they are hollow promises because it can't deliver on those promises (God intentionally made it unable to satisfy us); God's world doesn't look so appealing to our senses but it does satisfy the soul's deepest needs. Our world struggles under the curse of sin and death, and God has already passed judgment on it – its time will come; God's world remains untouched by that stain and therefore remains God's only choice for where spiritual life can be had.

Now here is this completely "other" world that we don't know anything about; we can, and do, live our entire lives in complete ignorance that it even exists. The two worlds actually run parallel to each other, like two cities on either side of a railroad track; and if it weren't for certain historical events that forced a link between the two we would still not know how the people lived "on the other side of the tracks."

One of the most important historical events that forged a bridge between the two worlds was the giving of the Holy Spirit. The Spirit reveals, makes plain, uncovers, makes "see-able" this other world that God lives in. It's like taking the veil away from a statue so that the public can see it for the first time. It's like opening a window into Heaven so that we can see inside.

The first occasion in the Bible where we find the Spirit doing this type of work is in connection with the Tabernacle. God was concerned that Moses and the Israelites build their central place of worship in the right way; not just anything would do. So instead of running the risk that the makers of the Tabernacle would misunderstand his instructions, no matter how plain he made them, the Lord poured out his Spirit on the two men in charge of the building project:

> See, the LORD has chosen Bezalel son of Uri, the son of Hur, of the tribe of Judah, and he has filled him with the Spirit of God, with skill, ability and knowledge in all kinds of

> crafts ... And he has given both him and Oholiab son of Ahisamach, of the tribe of Dan, the ability to teach others . . . so Bezalel, Oholiab and every skilled person to whom the LORD has given skill and ability to know how to carry out all the work of constructing the sanctuary are to do the work just as the LORD has commanded. (Exodus 35:30,34-35; 36:1)

And what did the Spirit show them?

> They serve at a sanctuary that is a copy and shadow of what is in Heaven. This is why Moses was warned when he was about to build the tabernacle: "See to it that you make everything according to the pattern shown you on the mountain." (Hebrews 8 5)

> The Spirit showed these men what the Heavenly Tabernacle, in God's world, looked like; to what extent we don't know, but at least we know that they saw the essentials so that they could pattern the earthly tabernacle after it in a way that would satisfy God.

> In Isaiah there is a prophecy of the Messiah, and it tells us that he will have the Spirit:

> The Spirit of the LORD will rest upon him – the Spirit of wisdom and of understanding, the Spirit of counsel and of power, the Spirit of knowledge and of the fear of the LORD ... He will not judge by what he sees with his eyes, or decide by what he hears with his ears ... (Isaiah 11:23)

> In other words, he won't rely on his senses to judge how to work in this world, but by what the Spirit tells him – knowledge from another world than this one.

Jesus said that when we face authorities who persecute us for our faith, the Spirit of God will give us the right words to say – words that we wouldn't ordinarily think of on our own. (Mark 13:11) He also promised to send the Spirit to us, who would "guide you into all truth." (John 16:13) The Spirit of God opened Stephen's eyes to see Christ standing at God's right hand when the Jews were stoning him. (Acts 7:55-56) The Spirit tells us what to pray for and how to pray when we don't know what to say. (Romans 8:26) The mystery of Christ "has now been revealed by the Spirit" to the Church." (Ephesians 3:5) Paul said that whoever rejects the teaching of Scripture isn't rejecting man but the Spirit, who is actually doing the teaching. (1 Thessalonians 4:8) The Spirit gives us a taste of the Heavenly gift, and enlightens us about the world of God. (Hebrews 6:4) The Prophets, Peter tells us, always spoke as they were "carried along by the Holy Spirit" – the Spirit told them what to say. (1 Peter 1:21) The Spirit testifies to the cleansing power of Christ's blood. (1 John 5:6) John the Apostle was praying in the Spirit when he had his revelation of Christ. (Revelation 1:10) The Spirit says things to the churches of Christ that they need to hear. (Revelation 2:11)

This is just a sampling from the Bible about the work of the Spirit as he reveals the world of God to our minds and souls.

- ***The Spirit gives power.*** "But you will receive power when the Holy Spirit comes on you; and you will be my witnesses in Jerusalem and in all Judea and Samaria, and to the ends of the earth." (Acts 1:8)

The kind of power that this verse is talking about isn't any power that we are familiar with. Simon made that mistake when he saw the Apostles working miracles and tried to buy the power of the

Spirit from them. (Acts 8:9-24) The power that the Spirit gives is a new thing, something that this world doesn't know anything about.

The first time that we find the empowering work of the Spirit in the Bible is in Genesis.

> In the beginning God created the Heavens and the earth. Now the earth was formless and empty, darkness was over the surface of the deep, and the Spirit of God was hovering over the waters (Genesis 1:1-2)

What exactly was there at the beginning, the building blocks that God used to make the world, we don't know; we do know that it was "without form" and "without substance" (as the Hebrew words mean), which are the two necessary characteristics of matter as we know it. In other words, the Spirit brought non-existence into existence; he gave life and substance to what used to be nothing. The earth and plants and animals and man all exist because the Spirit gave us the ability to exist. Without him we would return to nothingness.

That's what happened to the world when the Spirit moved in the beginning. What happens in men's souls? Here is where we need the Spirit most of all, because we are all dead to the world of God from our birth. (Ephesians 2:1-3) Even if we see God (the first job of the Spirit), and even if we know the truth about God and his world, we still can't do anything about it. God requires obedience from us – but we can't obey him because we are so bound up in our sin. He requires faith from us – but we can't believe in him because we are so confused, wandering in this dark world. He calls us to live in his world, but we can't get out of our world. At the very least we are to "love the Lord your God with all our heart and with all your soul and with all your mind" (Matthew 22:37), but unfortunately we aren't interested – there are other things that we love more.

When the Spirit works on the heart, however, that person wakes up to God's world, like opening one's eyes on a bright morning. "Wake up, O sleeper, rise from the dead, and Christ will shine on you." (Ephesians 5:14) He can see things now that he hasn't seen before. Even this dark world that we live in gets a new light: the Spirit shines on our lives, on circumstances, on other people, like a spotlight and shows us things that we couldn't see before.

The Spirit not only wakes us up to the world of God, he makes us *able* to live in God's world. "Flesh and blood cannot inherit the kingdom of God" (1 Corinthians 15:50), simply because the conditions there would kill us. The air is different, the food is different, the light is different (I'm using symbols of the realities, you understand; "air" and "food" and "light" in Heaven are spiritual things, whereas we think of our physical world when we hear those words.) Paul said that before we can hope to rise into Heaven, some things about us have to change:

> So it will be with the resurrection of the dead. The body that is sown is perishable, it is raised imperishable; it is sown in dishonor, it is raised in glory; it is sown in weakness, it is raised in power; it is sown a natural body, it is raised a spiritual body. (1 Corinthians 15:42-44)

In order to live before God and not die, we have to change completely. Our natures as they are now can neither survive before God's glory, nor can we understand or appreciate what we would see there. Our physical senses weren't made to be aware of the things of God. Unless, of course, the Spirit gives life to our souls – our souls *were* made to be aware of God. That's why the Bible talks about having "eyes to see" and "ears to hear." The Spirit makes us alive spiritually (which Jesus called, appropriately, being "born again" – John 3:3) so that our spiritual senses can start picking up on the things of God. In order to pick up the signals from a radio station, you have to first turn the radio on. Before anybody can hope to know God, their souls must be made alive first – by the Spirit.

The Spirit makes it possible for us to obey God's commands; without him we could never do it. (Ezekiel 36:26-27) The Law is spiritual, Paul says (Romans 7:14), and the Spirit shows us what God means by his Law and enables us to obey it. The Spirit of God blew over the bones in Israel and made them alive again. (Ezekiel 37:1-14) The Lord will build his kingdom "not by might nor by power, but by my Spirit" (Zechariah 4:6); because of this, his kingdom will be eternal and it will consist of things that will satisfy both him and us. Jesus drove out demons by the Spirit of God. (Matthew 12:28) Jesus said that, when someone has the Spirit in him, it will be a spring of water welling up inside to eternal life. (John 4:14) "The Spirit gives life, the flesh counts for nothing" (John 6:63) – and Jesus' words were Spirit because they give us spiritual life, the awareness of God and ability to live for God. Peter, the disciple whom the Jews had last seen denying the Lord, stood up at Pentecost full of the Spirit and preached the eternal Gospel to the Jews – with thousands of conversions as a result. (Acts 2) The Holy Spirit gives joy to God's people. (Romans 14:17) It's because of the Spirit's work that we have faith in Christ – a faith that comprehends the breadth and depth of Christ's person and work. (Ephesians 2:8; 3:16) The Spirit washes and renews us so that we become heirs of God's promises. (Titus 3:5)

Behind all other testimony

The Spirit is behind every other witness of God both in the Bible and in the Church today. If it were not for the Spirit, we would know nothing of God. Nobody has ever seen God face to face, and the only way that someone can experience anything from God is if the Spirit forms the link between him and God. "I declare to you, brothers, that flesh and blood cannot inherit the kingdom of God, nor does the perishable inherit the imperishable." (1 Corinthians 15:50) Until we die, we simply can't know God face to face. And until we actually step into Heaven at Judgment Day we will always depend on what the Spirit shows us about God.

Someone who testifies to us about God has himself seen God by means of the Holy Spirit. The Spirit opened his eyes to see the world of God, and hear the voice of God. That is, God revealed himself to the witness – the person didn't discover anything about God on his own.

And even while he tells us about it, the Spirit is helping him find the right words ("spiritual words" – 1 Corinthians 2:13) that will impress *us* with his testimony. Otherwise why would we believe what he said? They are only words, after all, that any person could say whether they meant them or not! It's a legal testimony that can be used against us on Judgment Day, but that doesn't mean much to many people either. What makes it penetrating is when the Spirit takes those words of a human witness and convicts our hearts with them. We know then that *God* is speaking to us, through this witness's words. Human testimony about God is valuable (as we will see later), but it depends completely on the work of the Spirit like a house depends on its foundation.

> We accept man's testimony, but God's testimony is greater because it is the testimony of God, which he has given about his Son. (1 John 5:9)

We can divide witnesses into two groups: the **primary** witness is the Spirit. He is the one who actually connects us with God, who opens our eyes to God's world, who opens our ears so that we can hear the words of God. The **secondary** witnesses are those who themselves experienced God (through the Spirit), and now they are telling us what happened to them. The primary witness can easily prove to us that God exists; a secondary witness can only testify to what God did for them. The primary witness has to step in and convince us of the truth of the testimony from a secondary witness – if he doesn't, the testimony of the secondary witness remains only words to us.

The Kingdom of God is a new world of new materials, built in new ways – and we're not at all familiar with this new world. We need someone to explain to us what's going on and the nature of the spiritual realities that we're dealing with. We need a "tour guide," an interpreter to help us understand this new world that Christ has brought us into. Even the Bible is pretty much a sealed book until the Spirit makes its mysteries plain to us. All of this requires the insights of the Spirit; he needs to reveal the meaning and depth of the work of God to us, while he does the work of God in our hearts.

The witnesses of the Bible understood how critical the Spirit was to their own testimony. As we have already seen, Peter told us that the Prophets didn't speak their own thoughts or words, but what the Spirit put into their minds – otherwise they wouldn't have been able to give us the truth. (2 Peter 1:20-21). For example, John was "in the Spirit" when he received visions of Christ and his coming kingdom. (Revelation 1:10) Here was a man who walked with Jesus for three years, and who ought to have been able to know anything about Jesus, without any outside help. Yet when God wanted to reveal certain crucial aspects of Christ to John, the only way that John could see those truths was if the Spirit opened up his eyes and enabled him to see.

John the Baptist saw the Spirit descend on Christ like a dove; this is an awesome thought in itself, because we would have thought that Jesus could easily do whatever he wanted to do – he knows all truth – without the "help" of the Spirit. Yet here he is being anointed by the Spirit at the beginning of his ministry! Evidently the Spirit was the source of his witness too.

Even those who have no interest in the things of God need the Spirit before they can prophecy. Balaam was hired, you will remember, to curse the Israelites; but when he arrived to do the work, he looked at them and "the Spirit of God came upon him" (Numbers 24:2) – then he uttered a prophecy that was totally different from what he originally intended! The Spirit is the source of truth, and if in God's will we are going to speak the truth, it *must* come from the Spirit – whether we are aware of it or not.

The link between the Spirit and the truth is so strong that the Bible itself is a product of the work of the Spirit. Without the Spirit, we couldn't rely on anything that the Bible says. But because the Spirit moved the writers of the Scriptures to say what they did, we can depend on the Bible to be the very words of God. It's nothing less than the pure truth, straight from God, unchanged by man in any way. We can know this is true because the Spirit testifies to us about what God has said:

> For the one whom God has sent *speaks the words of God*, for God gives the Spirit without limit. (John 3:34)

The Prophets and Apostles were filled with the Spirit when they wrote their books. Therefore they spoke only what they heard God say. There is an interesting verse in Hebrews that confirms this idea. The writer is developing his case that the old sacrificial system was only temporary, that God never intended physical sacrifices to cleanse the heart. To back this up, he says that "the Holy Spirit also testifies to us about this." (Hebrews 10:15) Then he quotes Jeremiah 31:33-34 to prove his point. In other words, he is saying that the passage that he quotes are the words of the Spirit (not of man) and therefore the words of God himself. How can he use any lesser authority when describing the priestly office of Christ? He has to be right about this! That's why he's careful to rely on *this* witness – the Holy Spirit – when making his case about Christ.

Finally, even *our* witnessing depends on the Holy Spirit. When Jesus sent the disciples out to witness about him, he told them what he would give them so that they would be able to do the job:

> But you will receive power when the Holy Spirit comes on you; and you will be my witnesses in Jerusalem, and in all Judea and Samaria, and to the ends of the earth. (Acts 1:8)

Think about this for a minute. These men had been with Jesus for over three years; they had many opportunities to watch him at work, to listen to his sermons and lessons, and even be specially trained by him for their work ahead. If anybody knew the facts of the life of Christ, they certainly should have. But they had to be filled with the Spirit *before* they could witness about him. Why? Because Jesus was such a mystery, even to those who were there and saw what he did first-hand, that no man can correctly understand him without the Spirit revealing the mystery to him. What were they going to tell people about him? That he did magic tricks? That he looked a certain way? That he seemed to do everything in a way that would insure failure? Many others who saw Jesus would say these things about him, but not the Apostles. The Spirit showed them the truth about Christ and told them what we, the Church, *need* to see in him to be saved. The Apostles saw the Son of God, the Lamb slain from the foundation of the world, the Messiah – and they skillfully opened up to us the things about Jesus that will save us. And this holds true for us also, when we witness to others about Christ. We can tell others the truth only if the Spirit has taught us, and made us skillful (through the gifts of the Spirit) in the spiritual art of making Jesus plain to those in need of him.

What the Spirit testifies about

You will notice that the Spirit steps in to testify when the subject at hand is too critical to leave to human attempts. God's world is beyond our physical senses; it should be no surprise that if we are to get the truth about Heaven, the treasures there, God's Law, judgment, reward and punishment – God has to tell us. The Spirit *reveals* what we could never have found out on our own. Unfortunately history is full of examples of people struggling to figure out what might be waiting for us after this life, and coming up with ridiculous and contradictory explanations.

Even though we need the testimony of secondary witnesses about God, that won't necessarily convince people. After all, to most people the Bible is just an ancient book – even to those who love it and learn it! If our knowledge of God remains only a tradition or teaching passed on from generation to generation – something that we received from others (although good in itself) – that doesn't convert the heart or instill fear and love of God.

What we need is the primary witness to press the truth home. He can and will bring us into the presence of this God that the secondary witnesses have told us about. There are certain things that we can't know for certain until the Spirit shows us. Then, when we've seen these things for ourselves, we are responsible: we are in a different legal position with God. He can hold us accountable now for what we've seen by means of the Spirit.

So, when we need to know the truth about the following spiritual areas, the Spirit himself steps in to explain things to us:

- **Creation** – We already noticed that the Spirit was the only witness present at the Creation event. (Genesis 1:2) This is important for several reasons: *first*, we need to know how the world came to be – that God made it, that he made it a certain way, that he gave man a job to do in his world, that it's "good" in God's eyes.

    Second, if it weren't for the Spirit telling us *how* God did it, we would never believe it. A witness tells us what he saw; and at Creation the Spirit watched God *command* his will into being, and the world came to exist – *all in six days*. This is important because we need to know what kind of a God we are dealing with here: he does the impossible, he works through miracles that nobody else can do or even understand. We are going to need this information later when we see him do the *same kinds of things* in the history of Israel, and in the ministry of Christ and the Apostles.

Third, the reason that the Spirit is testifying about what happened at Creation is because there was a lot more going on there than any human witness, no matter how skillful and faithful, could possibly pick up on. Believers usually read the first chapter of Genesis almost as if it were a scientific text, a step-by-step recipe explaining the beginning of the world. Under the surface, however, are spiritual issues that are astonishing. For example, do you realize what the command "Let there be ..." resulted in? A world of *servants*! Matter and energy *obeyed* the word of the Lord; in fact all things were created to obey him in their structure and purpose. God established himself as the Head and King over all his creation by the *way* he made them – by command.

God wasn't just interested in making a nice place for us to live. He made man, you will remember, in his image – which means that man reflects the nature of God in the way he handles himself in this world. That in itself is a high calling! We were made to rule: man's job was to bring God's Law and order over the earth. He was responsible to set up a peaceful and prosperous kingdom. He was to protect God's creatures from outside harm. The creation would be able to see God in our actions; it would feel his touch through us. And man of course was expected to lead all creation to the throne of Heaven in worship, praise, and giving God glory in all things. At the end of time God will judge us on how well we carried out that responsibility.

Another thing he had in mind (since he knew we were going to fail in our original calling) was to set up the new kingdom of Christ. With Genesis 12 God starts working on the Covenant, which is the solution for the sin and death that ruined the first world. The Temple, the sacrifices, the Promised Land, the covenant, the Son, the Church – all this requires a physical world, a "stage" if you will upon which to unfold his will. It's a spiritual kingdom, but first the Lord worked out the whole thing on a physical level so that we could understand what he was doing. The physical creation – and the nation of Israel in the Old Testament – was the womb, the cradle, of greater things to come in Christ. In his infinite wisdom God made the earth in such a way that we have a place to live and work *and* prepare for the second world.

Now these are things that we don't get if we read only the first few chapters of Genesis! The Spirit, who knew what God was doing at the beginning, gradually lets us in on the mind of God as the story of the entire Bible unfolds. By the end of the book we realize, if we have been reading attentively, that God had planned everything down to the last detail before he laid the first building block in the universe! For example, we are told that "he chose us in him [*that is, in Christ*] **before** the creation of the world to be holy and blameless in his sight." (Ephesians 1:4) We would never have known that God had all this in mind when he made the world (even after reading Genesis!), if it were not for the Spirit's witness in the entire Bible.

Why do we need to know these things about Creation? It makes the difference between a life lived for God and a life lived for self and pleasure. If God made the world to please us, and to let us do whatever we like here, then "Let us eat and drink, for tomorrow we die." There's no spiritual point to anything if that's true. But if he made us to glorify him, if he is steering history itself toward a spiritual goal, if this world is a stepping stone to the next one, and if what is done here in the flesh will have an enormous impact on our eternal existence there, then (if we aren't fools and reject the plain testimony of the Spirit) we must change our ways and do whatever is necessary to prepare for that day.

- **Christ** – As we have already seen, Christ is such a mysterious person that the entire world would have missed the point of his coming if someone hadn't made it plain to us what he was doing here. But this is one thing that we can't afford to be confused about! Here is our salvation, the wisdom of God, the Heir of the covenant, the Head of the Church, the King of kings, the second Adam, the Lamb slain for our sins.

So, when so much is at stake, the Spirit will step in as the key witness to make sure that we understand the truth about Jesus. For example, we first find the Spirit at Christ's baptism, where John the Baptist witnessed the Spirit coming down on Christ to initiate his official ministry:

> At that moment Heaven was opened, and he saw the Spirit of God descending like a dove and lighting on him. And a voice from Heaven said, "This is my Son, whom I love; with him I am well pleased." (Matthew 3:16-17)

Notice that as soon as the Spirit descends on Jesus, a revelation occurs: nobody would have guessed that this ordinary-looking man ("He had no beauty or majesty to attract us to him, nothing in his appearance that we should desire him" – Isaiah 53:1) was the Son of God!

There are four key areas in which the Spirit was working to reveal the true nature of Jesus Christ:

In Jesus' own person and ministry: There are two reasons that Jesus would have to have the Spirit of God working in his own life. *First*, Jesus told us several times that he did and said only what his Father in Heaven told him to do and say. (John 8:28-29) This may sound peculiar, that the Son of God who had all authority over Heaven and earth would be careful to obey his Father. But actually there's a good reason for it: he is the *same* God of the Old Testament now appearing in the flesh. This God does miracles; he always has. This God has profound wisdom.

> Coming to his hometown, he began teaching the people in their synagogue, and they were amazed. "Where did this man get this wisdom and these miraculous powers?" they asked. "Isn't this the carpenter's son? Isn't his mother's name Mary, and aren't his brothers James, Joseph, Simon and Judas? Aren't all his sisters with us? Where then did this man get all these things?" (Matthew 13:54-56)

> The people were amazed at his teaching, because he taught them as one who had authority, not as the teachers of the law. (Mark 1:22)

What the Jews saw was their God of the Old Testament within their reach now, where they could see and hear him for themselves. The Spirit of God gave this man the power of God to do the works of God. And the Jews should have known that this is the way their God would work, since the Prophets told them that God works "not by might nor by power, but by my Spirit, says the LORD Almighty." (Zechariah 4:6) With the Spirit of God, Jesus the man would do to his people what only God can do:

> Here is my servant, whom I uphold, my chosen one in whom I delight; I will put my Spirit on him and he will bring justice to the nations. (Isaiah 42:1)

Jesus, being the Son of God, already knew what God the Father was like, because he came from Heaven. As John the Baptist said of him, "The one who comes from Heaven is above all. *He testifies to what he has seen and heard*, but no one accepts his testimony." (John 3:31-32) Then, as if to hammer the point home about how one is able to know God and reveal that truth to others, he goes on to say this: "For the one whom God has sent speaks the words of God, for *God gives the Spirit* without limit." (John 3:34)

Second, Jesus is the model man, the way we all need to be if we want to live continually in God's presence. The Prophets told us long ago that Jesus would have the power of the Spirit upon him during his ministry, and that this accounts for the insights into God's spiritual world that made possible his life and teachings. That a man could do these things continually surprised everyone. But he promised his disciples that they would be able to do the same kinds of things themselves – because they too would have his Spirit, who would give them the power and wisdom from Heaven to do that work:

> I tell you the truth, anyone who has faith in me will do what I have been doing. He will do even greater things than these, because I am going to the Father. (John 14:12)

He showed us how a man must be filled with the Spirit, led by the Spirit, and empowered by the Spirit to solve life's problems. This is how all of God's children must live – totally dependent on God, receiving everything they need from him, through the Spirit working in their lives.

The revelation of Christ to others: Without the Spirit of God working in Jesus' life, everyone around him would never have gotten the point about him. He was, after all, born and raised in lowly circumstances. He never achieved greatness as this world measures it: he wasn't a king, or a soldier, or a successful businessman. In fact, he seemed to do things on purpose that made people look down on him and despise him!

This meant that if people were going to see him for what he really was, and understand his message, they would have to have their own eyes opened and their hearts changed. This is where the Spirit comes into the picture. To a people dead in sin, blinded by Satan and trusting in a superficial religion, Jesus was a constant source of revelation and surprises. Even to his own disciples he was a mystery until the Spirit drew aside the veil so that they could see the truth about him.

> When Jesus came to the region of Caesarea Philippi, he asked his disciples, "Who do people say the Son of Man is?" They replied, "Some say John the Baptist; others say Elijah; and still others, Jeremiah or one of the Prophets." "But what about you?" he asked. "Who do you say I am?" Simon Peter answered, "You are the Christ, the Son of the living God." Jesus replied, "Blessed are you, Simon son of Jonah, for this was not revealed to you by man, but by my Father in Heaven." (Matthew 16:13-17)

In order to believe in Jesus, we need faith – not common sense or logic or reason. There's nothing about Jesus on the outside, that we could get through our physical senses, that will help us understand him. The Spirit has to reveal Jesus to us; we have to be given a faith that looks past the outward physical form to the spiritual reality underneath.

We can see the effects of the Spirit working in Jesus, even if the text doesn't say specifically that it was the Spirit. For example, he opened up the true meaning and depth of the Law in the Sermon on the Mount – hate, he taught us, is really the same as murder, and lust is the same as adultery. Not that someone couldn't have guessed this on their own, but now they *knew* that God looked at things this way, and that these are the standards by which we *will* be judged on the Last Day. This reminds us again of what Paul says about the work of the Spirit – that "no one knows the thoughts of God except the Spirit of God." (1 Corinthians 2:11)

The Spirit of Christ in us now: Jesus wasn't done with the Spirit when he ascended into Heaven. The Spirit is so important as a link between us and God that one of Jesus' goals was to give us the Spirit too, so that we will know God for ourselves. He promised his disciples that he would make sure that we have the Spirit after he left earth:

> And I will ask the Father, and he will give you another Counselor to be with you forever – the Spirit of truth. The world cannot accept him, because it neither sees him nor knows him. But you know him, for he lives with you and will be in you. (John 14:16-17)

But what would the Spirit show us, once he took up residence inside us?

Before long, the world will not see me anymore, but you will see me. (John 14:19)

But the Counselor, the Holy Spirit, whom the Father will send in my name, will teach you all things and will remind you of everything I have said to you. (John 14:26)

When the Counselor comes, whom I will send to you from the Father, the Spirit of truth who goes out from the Father, he will testify about me. (John 15:26)

But when he, the Spirit of truth, comes, he will guide you into all truth. He will not speak on his own; he will speak only what he hears, and he will tell you what is yet to come. He will bring glory to me by taking from what is mine and making it known to you. All that belongs to the Father is mine. That is why I said the Spirit will take from what is mine and make it known to you. (John 16:13-15)

Now we can live in the power of the Spirit and experience the same kind of life that Jesus lives. We can live in the presence of God, we can seek God and find him, we can have the power and wisdom to resist the enemy, we can know that he hears our prayers and will answer them with the treasures of Heaven – all because of the Spirit of Christ living in us. The Spirit gives us a foretaste of what it will be like to live with God in Heaven:

I keep asking that the God of our Lord Jesus Christ, the glorious Father, may give you the Spirit of wisdom and revelation, so that you may know him better. I pray also that the eyes of your heart may be enlightened in order that you may know the hope to which he has called you, the riches of his glorious inheritance in the saints, and his incomparably great power for us who believe. (Ephesians 1:17-19)

The work of the Church of Christ: The Spirit is still working to reveal Christ to the world, through the members of the Church.

After Jesus had returned to Heaven, he sent his Spirit to the Apostles and the rest of the Church to make sure that the job of revealing the message, the depth, the love and presence of Christ would go on. The passages are too numerous to list here. For example, when he instructed the disciples about what to do next after his resurrection from the dead, he said that he would send them his Spirit so that they would witness about him:

> But you will receive power when the Holy Spirit comes on you; and you will be my witnesses in Jerusalem, and in all Judea and Samaria, and to the ends of the earth. (Acts 1:8)

Again, we see the purpose of the Spirit: to unfold the riches of the glory of Christ, because nothing less than the testimony of the Spirit will do the subject justice. Their work had to be backed up with the Spirit's work before it would actually change people's hearts. This is what's behind the gifts of the Spirit that are at work in the Church. Without the Spirit making the work of the Church powerful and effective, we would be wasting our time! And the whole point of the ministry of the Spirit through the work of the Church is to make Jesus more plain to everyone:

When the Counselor comes, whom I will send to you from the Father, the Spirit of truth who goes out from the Father, he will testify about me. (John 15:26)

Another example: when God wanted to show the Apostle John what would happen when Jesus came to destroy this world's kingdoms and set up his own everlasting kingdom, he did it through the Spirit: "On the Lord's Day I was in the Spirit." (Revelation 1:10) Because he was in the Spirit, he saw the glory and tremendous scope of the kingdom of the Son of God.

- **The Temple** – The Bible talks of at least five Temples. For each, the Spirit revealed the purpose of the Temple and what's going on there, because it isn't obvious to us otherwise.

You have probably read the sections of the Law that describe the **Old Testament Temple**: how it was built (down to the last detail!), the sacrifices that had to be offered and when, the priesthood, the ceremonies, and so on. To most people it's a complete mystery. It seems so pointless to fill up so much of the Bible with long descriptions of mundane matters like this.

But the Temple is of tremendous importance in the Kingdom of God. The Israelites knew that this was the only spot on earth where they could get forgiveness of their sins; what in the world would they do without their Temple? How could they live with their guilty consciences without God's system of sacrifice for sin? Plus, this was the only place where they could come into God's presence, since his throne was *in the Temple*. No other nation could claim to be able to come before the living God, as Israel could at her Temple. Even for those Israelites living far away from Jerusalem, they had to make the long journey to the Temple at least three times a year to worship there, in accordance with the Law – because there simply was no other worship allowed except at the Temple. Their God lived in Jerusalem.

Hebrews tells us the secret of the importance of the Old Testament Temple: it was actually built after the pattern of the original eternal, spiritual Temple that's in Heaven!

> They serve at a sanctuary that is a copy and shadow of what is in Heaven. This is why Moses was warned when he was about to build the tabernacle: "See to it that you make everything according to the pattern shown you on the mountain." (Hebrews 8:5)

There was a reason for this: the Temple in Heaven is where God lives, and the eternal sacrifice of Christ, planned long ago before the creation of the world, was the standard that the Israelite Temple had to conform to, in order to please God. God will be worshipped *his* way, not ours. When we go to Heaven and see him there surrounded by creatures who understand how to worship him, there we begin to realize how important it is to worship him in the right way. The earthly Temple had to be the same way.

But how can man know what goes on in Heaven? How can he know how to build the earthly Temple so that it matches the one in Heaven? The key is the Holy Spirit – he was the witness, the one who testified to the Israelites how God must be worshipped.

See, the Lord has chosen Bezalel son of Uri, the son of Hur, of the tribe of Judah, and he has filled him with the Spirit of God, with skill, ability and knowledge in all kinds of crafts ... And he has given both him and Oholiab son of Ahisamach, of the tribe of Dan, the ability to teach others ... So Bezalel, Oholiab and every skilled person to whom the Lord has given skill and ability to know how to carry out all the work of constructing the sanctuary are to do the work just as the Lord has commanded. (Exodus 35:30-31, 34; 36:1)

So the Spirit revealed the details of the Temple to the builders, so that they would build it to God's exacting specifications. The Israelites could be assured that if they built the Temple according to God's specifications, and conducted the ceremonies and services according to the Law, God would hear and be pleased with them, and receive them into his presence, and give them the blessings they needed.

The Spirit again served as a witness of Temple activities to the prophet **Ezekiel**. The Israelites, after centuries of playing games with God and worshipping both him *and* the idols of their pagan neighbors, were getting themselves in a dangerous position. God only puts up with our rebellion for so long before he draws the line. In this case, he was about to unleash one of the worst punishments he had ever inflicted on his people: to have the Babylonians invade the land, slaughter a large part of the population, destroy Jerusalem and the Temple, and haul the survivors hundreds of miles away into exile in Babylon. It was a punishment, as God put it, "that will make the ears of everyone who hears of it tingle." (Jeremiah 19:3)

But before it happened, God first performed a necessary ceremony at the Temple that only Ezekiel saw – and that's because the Spirit opened his eyes to it. You can read about it in Ezekiel 10-11. The glory of the Lord left from its place in the Holy of Holies, left the Temple premises, flew over the city of Jerusalem and went out into the hills away from the Israelites. It is perhaps the most solemn sight that a man has ever seen: God left his people to be ravaged by the coming enemy. Their protection was gone, and none of them knew it. The rest of the Israelites kept on worshipping at the Temple, offering sacrifices and prayers, while Ezekiel – who had seen what the Spirit showed him – knew that it was all in vain: they were worshipping a God who was no longer there.

Later, he also witnessed the return of the glory of the Lord to the Temple (Ezekiel 43) and was shown the plans for a new Temple when the Israelites would be restored from captivity.

We also know that **Jesus himself** was the Temple of God, as he claimed when he said –

> Destroy this temple, and I will raise it again in three days ... But the temple he had spoken of was his body. (John 2:19,21)

Since we have already seen that the Spirit's main purpose is to reveal the true nature of Christ, we can conclude that this also is one of the things that the Spirit will testify to: why Jesus is our Temple, how he resembles the Old Testament Temple, and how to take advantage of this situation.

Another Temple is the **Church**. We are the body of Christ; we are so united with him that the Bible says he is our Head and we are the body that he lives in. In fact, God is planning on living in us for eternity – in the same way that he lived in the Temple of the Old Testament:

> Don't you know that you yourselves are God's temple and that God's Spirit lives in you? (1 Corinthians 3:16)

> As you come to him, the living Stone– rejected by men but chosen by God and precious to him – you also, like living stones, are being built into a spiritual house to be a holy priesthood, offering spiritual sacrifices acceptable to God through Jesus Christ. (1 Peter 2:4-5)

> Now the dwelling of God is with men, and he will live with them. They will be his people, and God himself will be with them and be their God. (Revelation 21:3)

Finally, John was in the Spirit, remember, when he had the vision of the **new Jerusalem** coming down out of Heaven. There we have a detailed description of the new Temple – "I did not see a temple in the city, *because the Lord God Almighty and the Lamb are its temple.*" (Revelation 21:22)

Without the witness of the Spirit, people would inevitably get the wrong idea of the Temple and misuse it to their own purposes – and therefore miss the actual blessings that God wanted them to get from it. It's easy to miss the significance of the Temple. For example, the Jews thought that the Temple in Jerusalem was in itself their salvation – as if the blood of bulls and goats really could take away their sins. God assured them that it couldn't:

> "The multitude of your sacrifices – what are they to me?" says the LORD. "I have more than enough of burnt offerings, of rams and the fat of fattened animals; I have no pleasure in the blood of bulls and lambs and goats. When you come to appear before me, who has asked this of you, this trampling of my courts? Stop bringing meaningless offerings! Your incense is detestable to me." (Isaiah 1:11-13)

The Old Testament Temple was a symbol, a "type" of the Temple of Heaven. The blood sacrifices were a picture of Christ's blood that alone can take away our sin to God's satisfaction. But unless the Spirit opened the people's eyes to this truth, they would miss the whole point and go on in their meaningless ceremonies. This is true about the other Temples that the Bible talks about: without the help of the Spirit showing us what they really are and how they work, we can know nothing about them.

You can see, then, how the Spirit opens up the Temple of God for us clearly – so well that it helps us in our faith and work in the Church. We need this insight into God's Temple.

- **Our salvation** – At first glance it appears that salvation is a simple matter: just repent of one's sins, and believe the Gospel. From our point of view, it isn't any more difficult than that.

But if we are being led by the Spirit (as we should be, if we are truly converted – Galatians 5:18) we will soon find out that salvation is a huge matter. There's a lot to work on if we hope to be freed from our sins and reach our destination of Heaven. The Spirit is a faithful witness and intends to lead us into the fullness of our new life in Christ:

First, now we are alive to God. Before conversion, a person is completely dead to God – he can't know who God is, can't communicate with him, and must live in constant fear over his standing with God. But when the Spirit makes his soul alive to God, the line of communication is opened up and the relationship between God and man is restored. Now the heart can be fixed, and sin and death turned around to light and life.

Second, he shows us that we are God's children, adopted into the family of God, and heirs to the covenant of Abraham. This amazing revelation is the basis of all of our faith: knowing that we are welcome to God's throne, that he's our Father who loves us with the same love that he has for Jesus, and that the doors to forgiveness and mercy are open all the time.

Third, he puts the appropriate feelings in our hearts toward God and the world. On the one hand, we discover a love for God and the things of Christ that we didn't have before. We willingly turn our backs on this world, because it has nothing of interest for us now, and we want instead the spiritual Kingdom that we've been made alive to. Someone who doesn't have the witness of the Spirit in them can't understand why we're so willing to be "strangers and aliens" in this world – despising the things of the world, and putting our hopes and hearts on the next world!

Fourth, he shows us the inheritance that God has for us in Christ. There are vast – no, unlimited! – treasures in Heaven waiting for us in Christ. We are heirs of all that God has. It's a shame that so many Christians haven't seen this inheritance and started "laying up treasures in Heaven" as Jesus counseled us. Jesus truly is our "all in all," the fullness of God who has come within our reach, for our enjoyment and benefit. This is what we focus on in prayer.

Fifth, he opens our eyes to our brothers and sisters, the new family that we have been born into – the Church and body of Christ. Without the Spirit revealing our family relationship to one another in the Church, we of course will grow to hate others, judge them, despise and mistreat them – and focus on our own interests instead of what others need. With the Spirit, however, we will learn to "consider others better than ourselves."

Sixth, he lays out the weapons that God has given us to fight against the world, the flesh, and the devil. When the Spirit shows us how much power is in God's weapons, we understand how little use are the world's weapons. We of course have to train in order to get proficient in God's weapons, but over time we come to fully trust in what he has given us.

Seventh, he shows us how to worship God in a way that is mature and pleasing to God, even helping us when we don't know what to say or how to say it. God requires ceremony; he expects those who come to him to do so in a way that will glorify him and honor him. Worship has to be done a certain way. The Spirit shows us the throne room of God and instructs us on heavenly protocol; if we listen and learn, we can expect to get on God's good side and please him.

For a fascinating account of how the Spirit witnesses to us about these new realities of our faith, read Romans 8. We learn there how critical the Holy Spirit is to us. Step by step he reveals the essentials on how to live in the spiritual world of God, how to take advantage of those realities even while living in the limitations of this physical world. Here Paul talks of prayer, becoming holy, crucifying sin, receiving Christ's righteousness – and attributes it all to the work of the Spirit, who lights the way and shows us how to achieve all of this that was so impossible to people in the past.

Testifies to our spirits

The Spirit is unlike other witnesses in one important respect: he is in us, whereas we can only listen to the testimony of others through our physical senses. The words of others are just that: words. They may sound convincing, but it's possible to doubt their words. They say that they've experienced what they speak about, but we don't know that for sure. It's easy (though perhaps not reasonable) to question whether they are reliable witnesses. But when the Spirit speaks to our hearts, his testimony is so real, and convincing, that we can't deny it any more than we can deny our own existence. He can lift us into the presence of this God he testifies to. When the Spirit shows us the world of God and leads us spiritually down the streets of Heaven to the throne of God, we simply can't argue with the experience. We know that we are in touch with the living reality of God through the operation of the Spirit on our hearts. He reveals realities to us in a way that we are convinced of them.

How else will flesh and blood ever know God? God is Spirit, and we are physical. Adam was made with the ability to know God, but we (being born in sin) don't have that natural ability. We were born "*dead* in transgressions and sins" (Ephesians 2:1) – completely unable to know God or be aware of his spiritual world. If we are to communicate with him at all, we need a "bridge" between earth and Heaven, an open door through which we can get in touch with God. That bridge is the Spirit: being God, he can bring us into the very presence of God himself. Since he dwell in our hearts, he brings both sides together – God and man – so that we can live in the presence of God even while living in this physical world. We can experience the fact that God and his world are real. No other witness can do this for us, since they testify of what they lived through, but they can't take us back into that experience of theirs.

> As for you, the anointing you received from him remains in you, and you do not need anyone to teach you. But as his anointing teaches you about all things and as that anointing is real, not counterfeit – just as it has taught you, remain in him. (1 John 2:27)

There is one problem, however. It would be nice if, when the Spirit reveals the things of God to us – in fact, *proves* them to us spiritually so that we know for certain that such things are real – that we would accept his testimony and start taking advantage of the blessings in Christ that God has shown us. And sometimes we *do* believe what the Spirit tells us, but too often we are guilty of rejecting his testimony. There is never any doubt that the Spirit puts us in touch with the spiritual world, but often we decide we don't like what we see and turn our backs on it. We *reject* what the Spirit shows us. This is a particularly grievous sin, because we are rejecting what has been proven to us. It's possible to not believe a human witness because we may not be quite convinced that they are telling us the truth; but when God speaks to us directly, *there is no good reason to doubt him.* We know, just by the unique way that the Spirit works in our hearts (putting us in touch with the spiritual realities of God) that his testimony is true. This is why the writer of Hebrews warns us about resisting the witness of the Spirit:

> It is impossible for those who have once been enlightened, who have tasted the Heavenly gift, who have shared in the Holy Spirit, who have tasted the goodness of the word of God and the powers of the

> coming age, if they fall away, to be brought back to repentance, because to their loss they are crucifying the Son of God all over again and subjecting him to public disgrace. (Hebrews 6:4-6)

In fact, Jesus said that whoever rejects *his* testimony can be forgiven, but *not* if they reject the testimony of the Spirit!

> Anyone who speaks a word against the Son of Man will be forgiven, but anyone who speaks against the Holy Spirit will not be forgiven, either in this age or in the age to come. (Matthew 12:32)

It's a difference in the kind of testimony: Jesus' words were of a *man* (though he *is* the Son of God, he lived and taught as a man during his ministry – there's no denying that). But the Spirit's testimony is to the heart, connecting us in spirit to the reality that he speaks of. We listen to Jesus' words, and can accept or reject what he says, as many did in his day. But when the Spirit testifies to us, even with those very words that Jesus spoke first, he makes God real to us. So rejecting what the Spirit shows us is like turning away from someone we've been brought to meet, even as he stands before us and holds out his arms to accept us.

> If anyone sees his brother commit a sin that does not lead to death, he should pray and God will give him life. I refer to those whose sin does not lead to death. *There is a sin that leads to death.* I am not saying that he should pray about that. All wrongdoing is sin, and there is sin that does not lead to death. (1 John 5:16-17)

This is the unforgivable sin. Any other sin that we commit can be forgiven. Sin may take us a long way from where we ought to be, but God is always near us – he is always close enough to hear us if we turn and repent of our sin. If we call on him, he will hear us and answer, no matter what we've done. But when the Spirit has brought us to God and shown us the reality of Christ, and we don't want him – we turn our backs on him and refuse to call on him – of course there's no help for that. Unfortunately we often invent clever ways to turn a deaf ear and a blind eye to what the Spirit shows us; hence the warning of the Apostle – "And do not grieve the Holy Spirit of God, with whom you were sealed for the day of redemption." (Ephesians 4:30) To him, it's a grief when we refuse to live in the presence of the God we know. He was given to us just for the purpose of putting us together with God.

Since the Spirit lives in the heart of the believer, he is always ready to bring us into God's presence, by prayer and fellowship and the hearing of the Word. These are powerful means of grace that the Spirit uses to put us in touch with God. We need these, and we need the Spirit to bless our time spent in these activities, because otherwise our religion would turn into hearsay and ritual, impressive but not founded on anything spiritually real. For example, Paul said to "pray in the Spirit on all occasions with all kinds of prayers and requests." (Ephesians 6:18) The reason he said "in the Spirit" is because we have to come to grips with the reality of God when we pray; we have to see the things we want, and believe that God hears us and will answer us in Christ. "Without faith it is impossible to please God, because anyone who comes to him must believe that he exists and that he rewards those who earnestly seek him." (Hebrews 11:6) We *have* to know the reality of God in order to maintain our faith in him. The Spirit will always give us that sense of God's reality when we follow his leading.

The Witness of Christ

When Jesus Christ left Heaven and came to earth, he had a lot on his agenda, and a short time to do it all in. It's a proof of his divine nature that he took on the impossible – things that men and nations have been trying to do since the beginning of the world, and failed to achieve – and successfully accomplished his goals. Only the Son of God could have done what he did in one lifetime.

One important part of his ministry was to reveal the things of Heaven to us. This is why the Bible calls him a witness – "Jesus Christ, who is the faithful witness." (Revelation 1:5) There are many things that we need to be shown: the rewards that God has in mind for the faithful, the wrath of God that awaits sinners, the glory of God that transcends all human pride, the throne of God that controls all earthly governments, the warfare between spiritual powers over the earth, and many more things. Of course none of us have any notion that such things exist, since we don't have the benefit of having been to Heaven ourselves and seen those things firsthand. But Jesus, who is from Heaven, is determined that we know about these things; our eternal future depends on knowing the truth about them.

God within our reach

We saw how important the Holy Spirit is as a witness, but the witness of Jesus is different in one respect, in a way that particularly meets our own needs as humans. He became one of us. He took on flesh and blood and dwelt among men:

> Since the children have flesh and blood, he too shared in their humanity so that by his death he might destroy him who holds the power of death – that is, the devil – and free those who all their lives were held in slavery by their fear of death. For surely it is not angels he helps, but Abraham's descendants. For this reason he had to be made like his brothers in every way, in order that he might become a merciful and faithful high priest in service to God, and that he might make atonement for the sins of the people. Because he himself suffered when he was tempted, he is able to help those who are being tempted. (Hebrews 2:14-18)

> For we do not have a high priest who is unable to sympathize with our weaknesses, but we have one who has been tempted in every way, just as we are – yet was without sin. (Hebrews 4:15)

God is Spirit, and nobody can see God and survive the experience unless God keep him safe by a miracle. Even Moses, the servant of God, was only permitted to see the back of God as the Lord passed by him. (Exodus 33:21-23) So we have a serious problem: we won't be able to hear God, or see God, if we can't even get close to him! But by becoming a man, Jesus came down to our level, and now we can see God as he is, without fear of being overwhelmed with his holiness. Over time, the disciples gradually understood the amazing mercy of God in having Jesus come into the flesh where we can see him:

> That which was from the beginning, which we have heard, which we have seen with our eyes, which we have looked at and our hands have touched – this we proclaim concerning the Word of life. The life appeared; we have seen it and testify to it, and we proclaim to you the eternal life, which was with the Father and has appeared to us. We proclaim to you what we have seen and heard, so that you also may have fellowship with us. And our fellowship is with the Father and with his Son, Jesus Christ. (1 John 1:3)

The disciples themselves were witnesses of the incarnation of the Son of God, which we will look at later. But this God that they saw came within arm's reach, so to speak: he lived among them, ate with them, taught them, led them, comforted them, rebuked them – and in the entire experience they learned about what God was really like. It's one thing to read the words of a master in a book; but it's an entirely different experience to *live* with that Master. We can learn so much more that way, much more easily. Plus, he can be on hand to watch our progress and guide us in the way we need to go. That doesn't happen from reading a book.

Notice that the Bible calls Jesus the *faithful* witness – this means (in case there are those who tend to doubt him) that what he says, *really is true*. He is going to faithfully relay to us what he saw and heard in Heaven; we can depend completely on his testimony. In fact, Jesus repeatedly refused to do anything other than what the Father sent him to do. He was determined to speak only what his Father told him to say! That sounds confusing at first. If he really is the Son of God, can't he do whatever he likes and rightfully so? Yet there are many places in the New Testament in which Jesus claims the exact opposite!

> I tell you the truth, the Son can do nothing by himself; he can do only what he sees his Father doing, because whatever the Father does the Son also does. (John 5:19)

At first glance this seems strange, that he refuses to do anything on his own. Yet that's what makes his testimony all the more powerful: *There is only one God*, and therefore he does only what his Father tells him, so that we can know for certain what our God is like. There are not two Gods; the Jews learned that lesson very early in their history: "Hear, O Israel, the LORD our God, the LORD is one." (Deuteronomy 6:4) This is why they were so suspicious of Jesus' claims to be the Son of God. So when he spoke, and lived, and did miracles, he was careful to do it all *as their God* – nothing new, nothing different, nothing that would put any doubt in people's minds about the identity of the God they were seeing at work.

This means that, to the observant Jew, Jesus was revealing the God of the Old Testament. Watching Jesus at work, the Jew would have been reminded of the God who worked miracles in Moses' time, the God who made the covenant with Abraham, the God who called David to be king over Israel, the God who sent the Prophets to Israel, the God who punished the Israelites with exile, the God who brought his people back in mercy to inhabit the land. Jesus did the *same works*, and spoke the *same truths*, as the God of the Old Testament. He was testifying to the reality of the God that none of these Jews in his day had ever seen before. They had heard the stories, but now here he was in the flesh proving that he is very much alive and the same as ever.

Not every Jew realized what they were seeing, however. Their lack of faith in this very point is what prompted Jesus to rebuke Philip, for example:

> Don't you know me, Philip, even after I have been among you such a long time? Anyone who has seen me has seen the Father. How can you say, 'Show us the Father'? Don't you believe that I am in the Father, and that the Father is in me? The words I say to you are not just my own. Rather, it is the Father, living in me, who is doing his work. Believe me when I say that I am in the Father and the Father is in me; or at least believe on the evidence of the miracles themselves. (John 14:9-11)

To those who didn't have any faith – that is, they couldn't see the spiritual reality of Christ, and who he really was – he appeared only as the son of a carpenter, a poor man, an uneducated pretender from the country, a nobody, a trouble maker (to the Pharisees). There was no outward, physical reason to even respect him, let alone worship him.

> He had no beauty or majesty to attract us to him, nothing in his appearance that we should desire him. He was despised and rejected by men, a man of sorrows, and familiar with suffering. Like one from

whom men hide their faces he was despised, and we esteemed him not. (Isaiah 53:2-3)

But to those who had faith – the supernatural ability to pierce through the shadow veils of this world and see the reality of God's world – he appeared as the very image of God:

> The Son is the radiance of God's glory and the exact representation of his being, sustaining all things by his powerful word. (Hebrews 1:3)

> Simon Peter answered, "You are the Christ, the Son of the living God." (Matthew 16:16)

In other words, he was a living testimony of who God is, through his words and his life. The fact that he is the Son of God would have meant that whoever came near him would immediately realize that they were in the presence of God himself. People have never felt that way with any other man in history. When people met Jesus, they felt they were in the presence of God – their hearts "burned within them," their consciences smarted, they hid from him, they either loved him or hated him, they trusted him completely – all these were emotions that naturally arise when we are face to face with God. Others testified about God; but Jesus himself is a testimony that God is real, just by his very existence among us. That makes him unique among the witnesses of God.

There is a deeper power, however, in the testimony of Jesus than the Jews had in their Scriptures. Reading about God can give someone an intellectual understanding, and – during the times in the Old Testament when God was working among them – they could get a shadowy glimpse of what God was like. Doctrine and history do describe God to some extent. But there's a limitation to this kind of knowledge of God: it was based on earthly things, what the book of Hebrews calls the "shadows" of the reality in Heaven. For example, the Lord led the Israelites out of Egypt, showing them along the way the kind of physical power he had over Pharaoh, the Red Sea, and the Egyptian soldiers. This doesn't give us a full idea of his limitless spiritual power, however: the power that created the world, and the power that raised (for example) Christ from the dead. (1 Corinthians

6:14) Nor, when the Israelites heard the Law for the first time, did they realize the spiritual depth of the Law. For the rest of their history, they made the mistake of thinking that the Lord expected obedience on the outside, but not necessarily in their hearts. Jesus came to correct all these superficial notions of God. Here was God in person, in full power, in his glory – living and working in a way that would reveal to the Jews a deeper, more reliable, more useable model of the true God than the hints and promises of the Old Testament could give them.

This solves a deep-seated problem in our hearts. We are willing enough to believe in God who keeps his distance from us and allows us the freedom to live and work on our own, without interference from him. The Jews were happy to believe in a God of history – even a God of the Temple and the Law (which demanded outward signs of obedience). But Jesus brought the reality of God home to their hearts: he demanded love from them, he examined the fruit of their hearts, he expected them to renounce the world and follow him, he was impatient and not satisfied with their outward show of righteousness and religion, he knew the "thoughts and intents of their hearts." God presses his claim on us further than we dared to fear. Is God really like this? Does he really demand a total submission from us? Does he actually judge our thoughts and actions that closely, paying attention to every detail of our lives? That puts a whole new light on our relationship to, and responsibilities under, this God – if what Jesus showed us is true.

What does he show us?

Jesus will surprise us about what we thought we understood. We think that we know certain things about God, this world, and ourselves pretty well. But when Jesus opens up the real nature of the spiritual side of Creation, we begin to see things there that we didn't suspect before. The key is that he can enable us to see the world of God. He can work around our physical senses, and make the impossible happen. He actually draws us into the throne room of Heaven where we can see God in his glory (instead of having to guess or go by opinions). And from there we can also get a wonderfully clear view of what the physical world is really like.

Jesus is going to deal with matters of the heart. Perhaps we haven't been thinking along those lines before now, but his ministry opens up the heart so that we can be saved. He isn't satisfied with secondary issues – the things that we would rather study. He wants to save us from our sin, and deliver us from death, and make us fit for living in Heaven with a holy God.

With Jesus' testimony our Christianity will get put on an eternal basis. The poor Jews were so hopelessly mired in details of the Law that they couldn't see beyond this world. They missed the offer for a "Heavenly Jerusalem" because they were so wrapped up in the earthly one. Christians, on the other hand, who listen to Christ's testimony of a better world, will cut their ties with this world and start getting ready for the next world. They become "strangers and aliens" (Hebrews 4:13), unsatisfied with this world's treasures, and hoping for better treasures from their Father. And as we learn from Jesus the mysteries of the Gospel, we will discover that the Jews should have known about this spiritual world, or at least they had no good reason to reject it when Jesus offered it to them. Their forefather Abraham knew all about it! (John 8:56)

- **The Father** – The Old Testament is a big book (three times as big as the New Testament is!) but, in all of its pages, we can only find a handful of places that refer to God as the *Father*.[1] Jesus wants to testify about a truth that we find little of in the Old Testament: that God intends to adopt many children, that he has a rich inheritance for them in Heaven, and that he will bring them close to him in Heaven as his family – in a way that no other creature, not even the angels who have many privileges, will be allowed to participate in. Furthermore, God feels such a profound love for these new children that he forgives them all of their past and remakes them into his image.

---

[1] For examples, see Deuteronomy 1:31; Psalm 103:13; Proverbs 3:12; Isaiah 63:16; 64:8; Jeremiah 3:19; Malachi 1:6; 2:10.

There is no better example of his testimony concerning the Father than the story of the prodigal son – which, perhaps, ought to be renamed "the amazing love of the Father towards sinners." The son left home with his inheritance, spent it all in riotous living, and fell into misery and poverty after it was all gone. He came to his senses, Jesus tells us, and resolved to return home and ask for a job as a slave – since he didn't expect any good treatment from his (so he thought) offended father. He discovered an unexpected welcome, however:

> But while he was still a long way off, his father saw him and was filled with compassion for him; he ran to his son, threw his arms around him and kissed him. (Luke 15:20)

Not only was he forgiven for his sin, the father restored him to his former position in the family and showered gifts and honors upon him. This revelation of what the Father is like goes contrary to all of our expectations of him! How can he be *so loving* as to completely forgive and restore us? Can we really believe that he would do the same with us? Yet here is Jesus testifying to the most precious truth of the Gospel:

> For God *so loved* the world that he gave his one and only Son, that whoever believes in him shall not perish but have eternal life. (John 3:16)

If we didn't have his absolutely reliable witness of this great desire in God's heart, we simply couldn't believe it. Believe it, Jesus tells us: I know. I have seen the heart of the Father.

> No one knows the Son except the Father, and no one knows the Father

> except the Son and those to whom the Son chooses to reveal him. (Matthew 11:27)

What a revelation! He showed us the great lengths to which the Father is willing to go in order to save us. He did the works of the Father: he was sent under the commission of the Father, and he brought Heaven's power and resources to solve the problems of sin and death. He did miracles, knew the hearts of men and rebuked sin, taught the true depth of the Law, defeated the enemies of the kingdom, set up his own kingdom among his people and turned their hearts away from the world. In other words, he was here to start something real among men and women; not the shadows and promises that the Jews were still holding onto which couldn't save them, but the eternal kingdom that God intended to set up on earth from the beginning of time. Until then nothing had really worked to save people from sin and death. Jesus finally brought God's answer and started people's lives in real, permanent ways. In that he showed us God's amazing love which will never give up until we are saved.

> But when the time had fully come, God sent his Son, born of a woman, born under law, to redeem those under law, that we might receive the full rights of sons. (Galatians 4:4-5)

- **Our hearts** – "The heart is deceitful above all things and beyond cure. Who can understand it?" (Jeremiah 17:9) We think that we know ourselves very well, yet our knowledge of our innermost selves is more limited than we realize. All it takes is a tragedy in our lives to uncover whether we are living by faith or by sight. All it takes, in fact, are some circumstances that irritate us – someone crossing our paths, or denying us what we want – and immediately we react out of what we really are inside, not what we often claim to be. The fruit of our hearts can be ugly and embarrassing when others can see them.

Jesus knew that what we are on the outside doesn't often match what we are on the inside. He said once that he doesn't accept the testimony of man (John 5:34), and that's because we usually make great claims of being righteous yet live shameful lives of unbelief and sin. He has God's perspective on our hearts: he searches the heart of man, and tells us faithfully what he sees in there:

> I the LORD search the heart and examine the mind, to reward a man according to his conduct, according to what his deeds deserve. (Jeremiah 17:10)

It was unwelcome news to many, because they thought that they were pretty decent people – when really their hearts were reservoirs of wickedness and faithlessness that only wanted the right circumstances to be revealed.

> Don't you see that whatever enters the mouth goes into the stomach and then out of the body? But the things that come out of the mouth come from the heart, and these make a man 'unclean.' For out of the heart come evil thoughts, murder, adultery, sexual immorality, theft, false testimony, slander. These are what make a man 'unclean'; but eating with unwashed hands does not make him 'unclean.' (Matthew 15:17-20)

Notice how he has to correct their thinking about their hearts. This is the root of the value of a witness; he is someone who knows, because he has seen the truth and has faithfully passed on to us what he has seen and heard. Our only option is to believe his testimony; we cannot deny his words without saying that his eyewitness account is a lie – and God help us if we are so foolish!

One fatal flaw in our characters is this: we usually don't think that we need God's salvation. Most people do just fine (so they think) without Christianity, or at least with as little of the ceremony as they can get away with. But Christ has news for us:

> I told you that you would die in your sins; if you do not believe that *I am the one I claim to be*, you will indeed die in your sins. (John 8:24)

He knows something that we don't know. He can see – he has seen – the destroying angel sent from Heaven to strike down all those who are outside of God's appointed refuge. He can easily see if we are really safe from God's judgment as we claim. A general, for example, can walk around the camp and discern if the situation is safe or not, whether the troops are ready for battle. Jesus has looked us over carefully and is telling us, for our own good, whether we are spiritually ready for what lies ahead.

One place that you can read his testimony about heart matters is in the Sermon on the Mount – Matthew 5-7. As you will notice, he uncovers the real issues at stake: murder starts in the heart, adultery starts in the heart, obedience starts in the heart. There are many other Scriptures in which he testifies to what is in man's heart: the disciples were filled with pride, they were spiritually helpless before the enemy, they had little or no faith, they had little love for others, they didn't really have the spirit of forgiveness, they weren't humble, and so on. Being around Jesus is always a heart-searching experience! He can open us up like a book and make it plain to us what we really are inside.

- **The Law** – Let's go back to the Sermon on the Mount. In order to understand the purpose of this sermon, we have to know something about the background of those to whom he preached it – the Jews, the people of God, the descendants of Abraham, people of the Law of Moses.

The Jews were famous for keeping the Law, especially the Pharisees. For the last few hundred years they had analyzed every circumstance in life and found some way to apply the Law to it, in an effort to please God – or so they thought. They felt that if they could make everything they do satisfy some law, then they would be living righteous lives. The problem was, as Jesus points out in this sermon, that they were missing the whole point about the Law.

The only ones whom we will impress by keeping the Law through our actions is other people; we will not impress God with it, however. He knows that it's impossible to satisfy the real depth of the Law when we only work on building up a righteous exterior. We want to look holy to others who see our actions, while our hearts (which God sees) are actually pits of rebellion and wickedness. In fact, he gets angry when there's such a difference between our hearts and our actions:

> You brood of vipers, how can you who are evil say anything good? For out of the overflow of the heart the mouth speaks. The good man brings good things out of the good stored up in him, and the evil man brings evil things out of the evil stored up in him. (Matthew 12:34-35)

The Law was never meant to be a replacement for holiness of the heart, as if it's a veneer that hides what we really are inside. Using the Law like this offends God. He gave it out as a description of a righteous man – in this sense: a truly righteous man, someone who is holy *in his heart*, will live and act as the Law describes. That's why Jesus said things like "but I tell you that anyone who looks at a woman lustfully has already committed adultery with her in his heart." (Matthew 5:28) It doesn't matter that a man doesn't commit the physical act of adultery; if he lusts, then he's a Law-breaker *in his heart* and therefore subject to the penalty of the Law.

There are many passages in the Old Testament about the real meaning of the Law, which we don't have time to get into here. (For an example, see the real meaning of circumcision in Deuteronomy 10:16 and Deuteronomy 30:6.) Jesus testified to that spiritual level of the Law in his ministry; in fact, he surprised the Jews with his interpretation, but his testimony *was* true, nevertheless. He knows what the Law is about. After all, he is the Lawgiver! Who better to interpret the real meaning of the Law than the one who gave it to us?

For example, he wasn't changing the Law in any way when he told us things like the following:

> Love the Lord your God with all your heart and with all your soul and with all your mind. This is the first and greatest commandment. And the second is like it: Love your neighbor as yourself. All the Law and the Prophets hang on these two commandments. (Matthew 22:37-40)

He isn't changing the Law, he isn't setting any of it aside – rather he's showing us its true meaning, the reason it was given to us in the first place. Based on his testimony, we need to go back to the Law and learn more about it. We especially need to find out how we may have gotten such mistaken notions about it!

The Law was never meant to save us, or justify us before God. It was only a description of a righteous man, the outward evidences of a holy heart. *How* that heart becomes holy happens in an entirely different way than by following the Law, however. Jesus testified to this over and over too. He never said to put our hope in how well we have conformed to the Law's standards. He said, for example, that "unless your righteousness surpasses that of the Pharisees and the teachers of the law, you will certainly not enter the kingdom of Heaven." (Matthew 5:20) That's true – no sinner will be allowed into Heaven! And he ought to know: he made the "house rules." But *how* do we become so righteous? "If you do not believe that I am the one I claim to be, you will indeed die in your sins." (John 8:24) *Faith in Jesus* saves us from our sins; as we believe in him, we are delivered from sin and therefore become holy and fit for Heaven. Living by faith – and therefore following the Spirit – will result in a holy life as the Law understands that. (See Romans 8:4) But if we have no faith, we cannot be saved from sin, and we remain sinners – unfit for Heaven. Again, he ought to know all of this because he came for the purpose of saving sinners and making them righteous.

- **The Enemy** – One of the most important reasons Jesus came to earth was to destroy the devil's empire. Ever since the beginning, in the Garden of Eden, the devil has had his sway among men. It's time for that dominion over God's creation to end:

> The reason the Son of God appeared was to destroy the devil's work. (1 John 3:8)

The first thing to do, therefore, is to point him out: he names the enemy and makes him plain. Just his presence in this world brought out the devil into the light! When Jesus began his public ministry with a 40-

day fast, the devil came out in power to try to derail the plans of the King to destroy his enemy's works. "The tempter came to him" (Matthew 4:3) – an unprovoked attack, but entirely predictable, seeing that Jesus was here to cause havoc in the enemy camp.

The next thing to do was to reveal the enemy's main strategy. We might not have guessed what the devil's main weapon was; he certainly doesn't like his befuddled subjects to know what he's up to! But Jesus could see clearly how Satan held his power over us, and the time had come to reveal that strategy:

> You belong to your father, the devil, and you want to carry out your father's desire. He was a murderer from the beginning, not holding to the truth, for there is no truth in him. When he lies, he speaks his native language, for he is a liar and the father of lies. (John 8:44)

Satan works by way of lies: he deceives, he misleads, he leads us away from the truth of God to believe anything at all – just not the Bible! The world is filled with his lies, it relies on them, it will die by them rather than come to the knowledge of the truth. Satan has a grip first on people's minds, and from there their bodies and souls.

This should tell us something: break that hold on our minds, and we will be free of him. And that's precisely what Jesus taught:

> If you hold to my teaching, you are really my disciples. Then you will know the truth, and the truth will set you free. (John 8:31-32)

The truth is life, it's freedom, it's the primary weapon against the father of lies. He hates the truth.

That's why the demons couldn't resist him when he commanded them to come out of the possessed. Here was the Word of God incarnate, and devils have no resistance against him. Satan's eventual downfall is certain; Jesus testified that he saw the great victory:

> I saw Satan fall like lightning from Heaven. I have given you authority to trample on snakes and scorpions and to overcome all the power of the enemy; nothing will harm you. (Luke 10:18-19)

Now here is eyewitness testimony from someone who actually saw the weakness and end of Satan. And it's also a good example of how we can use the testimony of God's eyewitnesses to our own advantage: since Jesus assured us that Satan will be – has been! – overthrown, we have nothing to fear from any of his attacks. Our hope is in the living Word of God who protects us.

That leads to one last point – the prayer that Jesus offered up on our behalf. Just before he was crucified, he felt burdened to pray for our safety against the enemy:

> I have given them your word and the world has hated them, for they are not of the world any more than I am of the world. My prayer is not that you take them out of the world but that you protect them from the evil one. (John 17:14-15)

We can learn something here about another reality that Jesus sees: the protecting hand of God over us his children. To Jesus it's both real and necessary, otherwise he wouldn't have bothered to ask for it. This too should give us confidence, hope, and gratitude towards the Lord who has our well-being at heart. We may never see the danger over our heads, nor the warfare raging over us to keep the enemy away from us – but Jesus sees it all and has everything under control.

- **Heaven** – Unbelievers often make jokes about Heaven because, as we all know, we can't see it. It sounds like someone's imagination – people hoping that there's a better world after death because they have so many problems in this one. But Jesus assured us that there is a Heaven; he came from there, so he ought to know. So he proceeded to testify to what he had seen and known in Heaven.

In spite of what people think, we actually have a good deal of information about Heaven, and much of it came from Jesus' eyewitness accounts. For example, the best known passage is found in the Gospel of John:

> In my Father's house are many rooms; if it were not so, I would have told you. I am going there to prepare a place for you. And if I go and prepare a place for you, I will come back and take you to be with me that you also may be where I am. (John 14:2-3)

Jesus is revealing to us that there is a special place in God's own house for each of his children. They are expected, and they will be taken care of by Christ himself.

But there is much more about Heaven that we know because of Christ's testimony. For example, he goes on to say, in this same chapter, that *we know* the way to Heaven. He tells us what kind of people will be in Heaven. He tells us how people act in Heaven. He testifies that there are treasures there, waiting for the people of God, and tells us what those treasures are. He tells us what we will be doing there. He tells us who will *not* be there, and why.

Now these are only hints, because Heaven is of such a nature that we usually can't find appropriate words to describe such a spiritual place. Our experience is limited to earthly matters, and we don't have the minds or the words to fully know what Heaven is like. But the hints are enough to make God's children turn their backs on the pleasures and temptations of the world and hope for what Jesus describes.

But probably the most important fact of Heaven that Jesus testified to is this: **God is there.** That sounds rather elementary – of course God is in Heaven! But what staggering implications this simple fact has! Who is God? He is holy, he is a God of unfathomable mercy and grace, he is a God of vengeance, he is a God who sees the depths of the human heart and is not fooled by anything. If this is what God is like, then all of Heaven becomes one of two things: an agonizing misery to those who hate God, and an unimaginable joy and pleasure to those who love God. Whatever the wicked think Heaven may be, all we have to tell them is that the God of the Bible is there, controlling all things, giving all things, judging all things, getting glory from all things. And that's all we have to tell them – they want no part of it. The opposite is true for believers: when they hear that their God is there, the one who loves them and saved them, the one who promises to fill all their needs from his own table, the one who has been giving them tastes of that world already and revealing little bits of information about himself that gives them the strength and hope to persevere, then they *want* to be there for his sake, regardless of whatever else may be in Heaven.

- **Hell** – Jesus spoke more about this than you may realize. One would think that the Lord would spend all his time on happy themes, things that encourage us instead of discourage us. Especially when we consider how awful the concept is, we are surprised that Jesus would keep putting in front of us.

But you have to understand his motivation in this matter. The Law made it a special duty for the watchman to warn the people of coming disasters. The people in a city depended on the watchman. If he saw the enemy, then he must warn everyone – otherwise he would be guilty of their blood when disaster struck.

> But if the watchman sees the sword coming and does not blow the trumpet to warn the people and the sword comes and takes the life of one of them, that man will be taken away because of his sin, but I will hold the watchman accountable for his blood. (Ezekiel 33:6)

That's why Jesus warns us of the wrath of God, and shows us the means by which we can escape it. *Hell is an awesome reality.* It isn't a pretty subject – even God doesn't like the thought of it – but it's the appointed means of him getting glory from the stubborn rebellion of unrepentant sinners. It must be, and it *will* be.

Jesus always spoke of Hell as if he had seen it with his own eyes – which he had. So he is a witness of Hell; no matter what we think about it, he knows and he speaks from that knowledge. To contradict his testimony is the height of arrogance, even if we do it from humanitarian reasons. For example, here are some descriptions of Hell from Jesus' own eyewitness account:

> And if your eye causes you to sin, pluck it out. It is better for you to enter the kingdom of God with one eye than to have two eyes and be thrown into hell, where 'their worm does not die, and the fire is not quenched.' (Mark 9:47-48)

We get the impression that he wants us to do everything possible to avoid Hell! Evidently the place is so full of awe, so terrible to see, that he has come in urgency; not doubting that such a place exists – there is no time for such foolishness – but to warn us about it before it's too late for us.

> Do not be afraid of those who kill the body but cannot kill the soul. Rather, be afraid of the One who can destroy both soul and body in hell. (Matthew 10:28)

> The rich man also died and was buried. In hell, where he was in torment, he looked up and saw Abraham far away, with Lazarus by his side ... So he called to him, 'Father Abraham, have pity on me and send Lazarus to dip the tip of his finger in water and cool my tongue, because I am in agony in this fire.' (Luke 16:22-24)

Many people are offended whenever they read Jesus' description of Hell. But that's being foolish; instead, they should take advantage of the warning. Jesus is doing what any decent person would do who has seen the potential for disaster.

> Rescue those being led away to death; hold back those staggering toward slaughter. If you say, 'But we knew nothing about this,' does not he who weighs the heart perceive it? Does not he who guards your life know it? Will he not repay each person according to what he has done? (Proverbs 24:11-12)

- **The way of life** – We mentioned before that Jesus had to debunk the popular conception that the Law is a sinner's hope. Trying to follow the Law will *not* get us eternal life. Not that there is anything wrong with the

Law – Jesus said, "Do not think that I have come to abolish the Law or the Prophets; I have not come to abolish them but to *fulfill* them." (Matthew 5:17) The problem isn't with the Law; the problem is with us.

Nobody can fulfill the Law perfectly, except Jesus himself. When one young man rashly claimed that he had fulfilled the Law perfectly, Jesus felt bound to prove otherwise through a clever technique: "If you want to be perfect, go, sell your possessions and give to the poor, and you will have treasure in Heaven. Then come, follow me." (Matthew 19:21) The man couldn't do it, which means that he was using the Law in a superficial way; in his heart he was not a holy man.

What is the way to life, then? Jesus knew. He saw, and was following, the only way to eternal life. He testified to what he saw and knew. For example, he told the Jews that "I am going away, and you will look for me, and you will die in your sin. Where I go, you cannot come." (John 8:21) Unless they accepted his testimony and acted on it, they would never find the way to life.

> If anyone would come after me, he must deny himself and take up his cross and follow me. For whoever wants to save his life will lose it, but whoever loses his life for me will find it. (Matthew 16:24-25)

This sounds like he's leading to death instead of life! A cross means death to this world: to our old friends, our old lifestyles, our old likes and dislikes. We will become dead to all that we used to be and enjoy. But that's the necessary first step to life with God. According to the testimony of Jesus, death comes first – and that gives way to life.

> I tell you the truth, unless a kernel of wheat falls to the ground and dies, it remains only a single seed. But if it dies, it produces many seeds. The man who loves his life will lose it, while the man who hates his life in this world will keep it for eternal life. (John 12:24-25)

Even though he continually spoke of the way of life, his disciples were often confused and didn't understand what he was talking about. Once when he told them that "you know the way to the place where I am going" (John 14:4), they claimed that they didn't. Then he told them plainly:

> I am the way and the truth and the life. No one comes to the Father except through me. (John 14:6)

Now think through this for a minute. The way to life is Jesus himself. What is he, then? He is our King, our Lord – and whatever he commands is designed to lead us to life. He is our Wisdom – and whatever he says is the truth, and it works. He is our Light – being around him means that we see things as they really are. He is our High Priest – he is our Righteousness – he is our Bread from Heaven – he is our Shield from our enemies, and on and on the names of Jesus go. He is literally everything that we could ever possibly want or need, spiritually speaking. That's why Jesus said that it's *him* that we need:

> Whoever eats my flesh and drinks my blood has eternal life, and I will raise him up at the last day. For my flesh is real food and my blood is real drink. Whoever eats my flesh and drinks my blood remains in me, and I in him. (John 6:54-56)

- **The world** – Being from outside the world gave Jesus a perspective on it that is difficult for us to get on our own. We are so much a part of it – we can't see our own faces unless we look in a mirror, and we can't really understand the true nature of the world we live in unless someone shows it to us. But it was easy for Jesus to see the many problems and pitfalls of the world. Part of his witness, then, was to tell us all about those things.

"In this world you will have trouble." (John 16:33) And he knows! He didn't come naïvely into this world of sin and rebellion and death. Nobody caught him unawares of what is really going on here. He came to destroy death, to destroy the dominion of the one with the power of death: "The reason the Son of God appeared was to destroy the devil's work." (1 John 3:8) He knew what was in the hearts of sinful men, and that they wouldn't believe his testimony. He knew that his own disciples would fail him! He came into this problematic world with his eyes open – ready to set the process in motion to *change* the world.

Jesus warned the disciples that they would experience the same kind of treatment from the world that he got, if they followed him faithfully.

> If the world hates you, keep in mind that it hated me first. If you belonged to the world, it would love you as its own. As it is, you do not belong to the world, but I have chosen you out of the world. That is why the world hates you. (John 15:18-19)

Now this isn't the world he created – God *loved* the world he made, and wants to redeem it from death to life. The world that Jesus hates and is determined to destroy is the *world system*: the conscious rebellion of man and devil against God's commands, the system that trains each new generation of children in the ways of sin and death, the glitter and pomp and false promise that leads us to think that we can be satisfied with a life *without God*. It is worldwide, it is firmly entrenched in every age, and it's killing us spiritually.

When Jesus prayed to the Father, he pleaded for help about this very point. He knew that we had to stay here, in the world, subject to its temptations and sufferings. He knew that we don't have much of a chance fighting against a worldwide system that we are so used to already. He knew that it would take the power of God, like a shield around us, to protect us from the world while we continue living in the world.

> I have given them your word and the world has hated them, for they are not of the world any more than I am of the world. My prayer is not that you take them out of the world but that you protect them from the evil one. They are not of the world, even as I am not of it. (John 17:14-16)

In order to guide us through the world with the least amount of damage done spiritually, he counseled us about ways that he knew – like a scout sent to lead the main army through enemy territory. The point is that these aren't just wise sayings he came up with; he saw and knew these paths. He was an eyewitness to them. We have to accept his testimony about these ways or else we'll get lost. For example, he told the rich young man to sell his possessions and give to the poor. He told another man to leave his unburied father behind. He told others to take up their crosses. Once he said something that, surely, makes the hearts of modern believers tremble!

> Use worldly wealth to gain friends for yourselves, so that when it is gone, you will be welcomed into eternal dwellings. (Luke 16:9)

He knew that this leads to eternal life! He also knows that riches and wealth and prestige and honors are a stumbling block for people.

> The one who received the seed that fell among the thorns is the man who hears the word, but the worries of this life and the deceitfulness of wealth choke it, making it unfruitful. (Matthew 13:22)

> No one can serve two masters. Either he will hate the one and love the other, or he will be devoted to the one and despise the other. You cannot serve both God and Money. (Matthew 6:24)

The world is full of pitfalls, unfortunately, which is why most don't ever find the way to life.

> Enter through the narrow gate. For wide is the gate and broad is the road that leads to destruction, and many enter through it. But small is the gate and narrow the road that leads to life, and only a few find it. (Matthew 7:13-14)

The point here is that we don't know the thousandth part of the dangers, deceits, and miseries that this world contains. We need the testimony of someone who *can* see, who knows what the world is, and who can advise us on how to avoid trouble.

- **The Kingdom of God** – Jesus taught a great deal about the Kingdom of God, primarily because he's the King and he came here to lay the foundations for it! If he wouldn't have said anything about it, we never would have known that, right under our noses, a new world is being built that will one day take the place of the world we live in now. But because God is merciful, Jesus taught us about this new world and showed us how to get into it.

The first creation fell into ruin because of the sin of man; we ruined the world with our rebellion, and we're still "re-creating" God's original world to suit ourselves. The world we've come up with is filled with sin, death, frustration, rebellion, and ignorance. It isn't at all like the world that God originally had in mind. We shouldn't be surprised, then, to find out that God has plans to destroy it all and make a new one.

The new Kingdom, however, isn't going to be like the first one. This is what Jesus' mission was: to teach us what God's new world would be like. Jesus has seen the plans, was here on earth himself to lay the foundations for it, and is presently building it block by block out of eternal stone. His testimony, therefore, should be utterly reliable.

What will it be like? Jesus told us many characteristics of this Kingdom – which we find especially in the "Kingdom parables."

> The kingdom of Heaven is like a mustard seed, which a man took and planted in his field. Though it is the smallest of all your seeds, yet when it grows, it is the largest of garden plants and becomes a tree, so that the birds of the air come and perch in its branches. (Matthew 13:31-32)

> The kingdom of Heaven is like yeast that a woman took and mixed into a large amount of flour until it worked all through the dough. (Matthew 13:33)

> The kingdom of Heaven is like treasure hidden in a field. When a man found it, he hid it

again, and then in his joy went and sold all he had and bought that field. (Matthew 13:44)

Again, the kingdom of Heaven is like a merchant looking for fine pearls. When he found one of great value, he went away and sold everything he had and bought it. (Matthew 13:45-46)

The reason he's telling us these things is that it's easy to miss the Kingdom of Heaven! We don't have spiritual eyes to see such a place, even though it's growing up all around us. Plus, our whole lives center around this physical world, and we aren't used to – or perhaps aren't interested in – looking for another world besides this one. But to Jesus it's like two sides to a railroad track: he can see both sides clearly, even when we're blind to what's on the other side. And he will point out to us the particularly difficult things to understand about the Kingdom of Heaven, because it's precisely those things that will save us.

He also taught us why we need a new Kingdom. We already looked at how faithfully he pointed out the presence and work of the enemy; what we need to be convinced of, however, besides this is that the enemy has destroyed our world and our own lives. There is nothing here to live for; it's all ruined, souls are lost, people are devoid of even the common grace of morality, and nobody cares. The enemy has done a remarkable job of turning God's Paradise into a blasted war zone. What we need now is a new King, a new government, a new way of achieving and keeping righteousness, and a new value system.

Jesus also pointed out the fact that he's the new King. He is going to be a tough King to serve – his rules are far more stringent than the Jews thought their God would be. For example, Jesus assured us that in his Kingdom even those who lust will be punished as adulterers! He makes it very plain what will happen to the wicked: he said, for instance, that it would be better that those who mistreat the children of God would be better off thrown into the ocean with a huge millstone tied around their necks. The righteous, he assured us, will receive a hero's welcome into the Kingdom – even though most of them will be the world's nobodies. Strange things will happen in this Kingdom. But we can know what things will be like, if we listen to his testimony about it.

The proof of Jesus' testimony

We have seen that the testimony of Jesus is of tremendous scope: he not only knows a great deal about what's in God's world, he knows its true nature. He tells us what we will find there, as well as how to use it to our advantage. And he knows us quite well, which is why he knows what to tell us – the things we need to be saved.

There is just one problem, however. It *is* possible not to believe the testimony of Jesus. They are, after all, only words, and we don't always believe what we hear. In fact, the testimony that he gave in his day was so incredible that very few people believed him. The Pharisees certainly didn't! Even his disciples found it hard to believe. When he told them that he had to go to Jerusalem to be killed, Peter drew him aside and rebuked him for such talk!

> Peter took him aside and began to rebuke him. "Never, Lord!" he said. "This shall never happen to you!" Jesus turned and said to Peter, "Get behind me, Satan! You are a stumbling block to me; you do not have in mind the things of God, but the things of men." (Matthew 16:22-23)

You can see how Jesus reacts to people not believing him: very harshly. When we doubt him, it's the same thing as calling him a *liar*. And naturally he won't take that from anybody, especially from his own people.

But he does know that people aren't going to believe him. If we need proof, history has shown us that. The things he taught, the lifestyle he expected of his people, are things that generations have rejected as unreasonable and against common sense. People despised him and still do – even using his name as a curse word! He came in humility as a nobody, and he's still treated as a nobody, as if his claim to be King over all the earth means nothing at all.

In order to see the truth in Jesus and accept his testimony, we have to have *faith*. Not a blind hope, or a gut instinct that everything will turn out in the end. It has to be a true vision of Heaven's treasures – a spiritual verification that everything Jesus talked about is absolutely true. Without that confirming faith we will never believe his testimony.

In showing the peculiar position we're in about whether to believe what Jesus taught us, he compared his own testimony to that of the Spirit:

> Anyone who speaks a word against the Son of Man will be forgiven, but anyone who speaks against the Holy Spirit will not be forgiven, either in this age or in the age to come. (Matthew 12:32)

Jesus' witness, even though it's the truth and must not be questioned, *can* be questioned – they *are* only words. The Spirit's testimony, however, (as we've already seen) are those same words of Jesus pressed home into the heart so that we know the reality behind them. We can be forgiven for not believing Jesus (if we come to him and repent of our unbelief!); as he said once of those crucifying him, "Father, forgive them, for they do not know what they are doing." (Luke 23:34) But those who refuse to believe the Spirit are flying in the face of what they have seen, and heard, from Heaven itself.

There is one aspect of Jesus' testimony that obligates us to believe it, however, even though it sounds incredible: he worked miracles in order to convince us that he was telling us the truth. The idea is this: anybody who could do these miracles *must* be from God and he must know what he is talking about. Others said this about him, and he himself claimed that as his motivation for doing the miracles.

> Do not believe me unless I do what my Father does. But if I do it, even though you do not believe me, believe the miracles, that you may know and understand that the Father is in me, and I in the Father. (John 10:37-38)

And another time, when John the Baptist sent his men to Jesus to see if he really was the Christ, Jesus responded by pointing them to the miracles:

> Go back and report to John what you hear and see: The blind receive sight, the lame walk, those who have leprosy are cured, the deaf hear, the dead are raised, and the good news is preached to the poor. (Matthew 11:4-5)

In other words, his ministry of miracles supported his ministry of testimony. Only God can do such things, so that should lend credibility to everything he says. That doesn't always work, however, because there are those who are obstinate in their unbelief and even the miracles won't convince them.

> The miracles I do in my Father's name speak for me, but you do not believe because you are not my sheep. (John 10:25-26)

> If they do not listen to Moses and the Prophets, they will not be convinced even if someone rises from the dead. (Luke 16:31)

The Testimony of God

One final point. Even though we said that Jesus' testimony was just words, we have to understand that they are the *words of God*

– and therefore of a quality that is far superior to the words of men. What he said is the truth come out of Heaven.

> Don't you believe that I am in the Father, and that the Father is in me? The words I say to you are not just my own. Rather, it is the Father, living in me, who is doing his work. (John 14:10)

The source of someone's information is one important factor on how seriously we should take his testimony. A gullible or ignorant witness will tell us what he was deceived into thinking. But a person who knows where to get the latest and best information is a reliable witness. Jesus claimed that his words were God's words – which is the highest and most reliable authority we could possibly ask for! We may not want to believe this claim of his, but it's still impressive. As has been often observed, he's either the boldest liar in history or he really is the Word of God.

If he were merely a man, we would do well to check his testimony against the testimony of others. But we don't need to check his; who else would we go to to verify the words of God himself? Human testimony is a derived testimony: we get our information from the Spirit, and we pass on what we've learned to others. But Jesus testifies about himself, and we can't easily challenge that testimony because he knows himself perfectly:

> In your own Law it is written that the testimony of two men is valid. I am one who testifies for myself; my other witness is the Father, who sent me. (John 8:17-18)

Jesus sees things from his own unique point of view: he's the Creator, the Redeemer, the King of the universe, the Provider, the Judge of all the earth. Naturally his perspective on things is unquestionable. He's just as powerful and as key a witness as the Holy Spirit is. We have no choice but to believe his testimony.

The Witness of the Prophets

The Prophets aren't very well understood by modern students, probably because we bring our own misconceptions to their writings that keep us from really hearing what they were saying. We like to study the prophecies concerning Christ, and we also like to try to figure out how the world will end (called **eschatology**, of which we have many theories – all supported by the Prophets, supposedly!). But the Prophets were witnesses to a bigger reality, of which these individual aspects of prophecy are only parts; they saw a world that encompasses them all and much more. They not only knew that Christ *would* come – they knew *who* Christ was and *why* he was coming!

The Word of the Lord

What is a prophet? Most people think that a prophet is someone who 1) predicts the future, and 2) confronts us with the Word of God. This is true, but a Biblical prophet does more than that. If he only predicted the future, then so-called seers of any religion would be prophets – but God won't claim *them*. Predicting the future, in itself, is no sign that God sent someone to us. Even if his words came true, that's still not proof that he was sent by God.

> If a prophet, or one who foretells by dreams, appears among you and announces to you a miraculous sign or wonder, and if the sign or wonder of which he has spoken takes place, and he says, "Let us follow other gods" (gods you have not known) "and let us worship them," you must not listen to the words of that prophet or dreamer. The LORD your God is testing you

to find out whether you love him with all your heart and with all your soul. It is the LORD your God you must follow, and him you must revere. Keep his commands and obey him; serve him and hold fast to him. That prophet or dreamer must be put to death, because he preached rebellion against the LORD your God, who brought you out of Egypt and redeemed you from the land of slavery; he has tried to turn you from the way the LORD your God commanded you to follow. You must purge the evil from among you. (Deuteronomy 13:1-5)

And if a man confronts us with God's Word, how is that different from modern preachers and teachers, who also confront us with God's Word? Yet preachers don't *know* the state of our hearts; they preach in hope and faith that the message that God gave them will be used by God for our good. The Biblical Prophets, however, *knew* the hearts of their hearers: God showed them. They knew that their words were directed to specific individuals, for specific sins. There was no guessing or hoping involved.

A prophet was also known as a "seer" – which just means that he saw things that other people couldn't see.

> Formerly in Israel, if a man went to inquire of God, he would say, "Come, let us go to the seer," because the prophet of today used to be called a seer. (1 Samuel 9:9)

What did he see? It doesn't require a prophet to be able to see things in the physical world; therefore the Prophets saw *God's* world. They were enabled by the Spirit to see God on his throne, directing the affairs of nations, judging the hearts of men, and saving his people. These are things that ordinarily are hidden from the eyes of flesh. For example, these prophecies demonstrate that the Prophets saw and heard God:

> In the year that King Uzziah died, I saw the Lord seated on a throne, high and exalted, and the train of his robe filled the temple. (Isaiah 6:1)

> This was the appearance of the likeness of the glory of the LORD. When I saw it, I fell facedown, and I heard the voice of one speaking. (Ezekiel 1:28)

> Since then, no prophet has risen in Israel like Moses, whom the LORD knew face to face, who did all those miraculous signs and wonders the LORD sent him to do in Egypt – to Pharaoh and to all his officials and to his whole land. For no one has ever shown the mighty power or performed the awesome deeds that Moses did in the sight of all Israel. (Deuteronomy 34:10-12)

The reason we have to stress this is because many modern scholars doubt that the Prophets of the Bible really saw God or heard his voice. They don't believe in direct inspiration; they feel that the Prophets actually formed their prophecies from their own minds, guided by some subconscious feelings that managed to pick up on historical trends and the religious feelings of the nation. The Prophets, these scholars teach, actually helped to *create* the Israelite religion as it developed through history from Moses to Malachi.

But all the Prophets saw or heard God directly. They didn't make up a thing. The mystery of God and his ways are hidden to the mind of man, and none of us – even if we're masters of the religion that God has given us so far – can guess what God will say next. The Prophets found themselves in the presence of God and able to see things that neither they nor anybody else had known, or had any chance of knowing. And Peter tells us why they were able to see the things of God:

> Above all, you must understand that no prophecy of Scripture came about by the prophet's own interpretation. For prophecy never had its origin in the will of man, *but men spoke from God as they were carried along by the Holy Spirit.* (2 Peter 1:30-21)

The Holy Spirit, who reveals the things of God to us, opened the doors of Heaven so that the Prophets could see inside. The Spirit opened the ears of the Prophets so that they could hear the words that God spoke to them. There was never any doubt in their minds that this was the case, which is why they said things like "Thus says the Lord." They knew that none of this was of their own doing or imagination.

Their information came in various ways – through visions, hearing God's voice, an inner leading, miracles, etc. "In the past God spoke to our forefathers through the Prophets at many times and in various ways." (Hebrews 1:1) And probably those "various ways" by which they saw God have led to today's confusion about the Prophets' own part in the process. We all have religious feelings and opinions concerning social justice, and morality. We naturally would believe that a strongly religious man in Israel's history would have had his own opinions on how faithfully the religion of Yahweh was practiced from the palace on down through the rest of society. How can we be certain, then, that a prophet didn't formulate his sermon in exactly the same way as modern preachers do – thinking about the Word, finding his own words to express his strong feelings, and addressing the situation of his hearers as he thought best?

But there's the point: we *can* know how they got their information – *they told us how*.

The word of the LORD came to Abram in a vision:
(Genesis 15:1)

Then the word of the LORD came to Samuel:
(1 Samuel 15:10)

That night the word of the LORD came to Nathan, saying: (2 Samuel 7:4)

For I was commanded by the word of the LORD:
(1 Kings 13:9)

Then the word of the LORD came to Elijah the Tishbite:
(1 Kings 21:17)

Then the word of the LORD came to Isaiah:
(Isaiah 38:4)

The word of the LORD came to me, saying: (Jeremiah 1:4)

The word of the LORD came to Ezekiel the priest:
(Ezekiel 1:3)

The word of the LORD that came to Hosea:
(Hosea 1:1)

The word of the LORD that came to Joel son of Pethuel:
(Joel 1:1)

The word of the LORD came to the prophet Zechariah:
(Zechariah 1:1)

These are only a few of the passages that plainly state how the Word of God came to the Prophets. Each one is followed by a *quotation* direct from God, not their own religious feelings. Why do we stress this point? Because what the prophet says has the greatest weight and authority among men as *the Word of God*, not the words of men, and we *must* listen to what they say if we want to know the truth. They are not making things up, they are not teaching man's wisdom or making modern applications for ancient ideas. Their words are, plainly and simply, **God's words**.

The Prophets were witnesses of God. They were brought into his presence, they saw his glory, they heard him speak, they watched God's activities in Heaven and his works on earth. They are reporting to us what they saw for themselves – things that we in our day have never seen or heard. If it weren't for the fact that we have this testimony of a reality that puts our world – and our lives – in a whole new light, we would never believe it. The message is so startling, in fact, that people don't believe it; they don't want to believe it.

That's why God made the Prophets eyewitnesses, to refute the arguments of the critics. It's the fashion in scholarly circles nowadays to consider much of the message of the Prophets as myths and fairy tales, or religious imagination and creativity. They don't believe that the Prophets spoke the actual words of God, and they have scholarly reasons for their unbelief. But what it amounts to is this: they are calling a lot of God's special messengers *liars*. And if the Prophets claimed to be speaking God's words, then the words themselves – which many scholars doubt – must be lies too. Therefore the skeptics fall under the category that John mentions:

> Anyone who does not believe God has made him out to be a liar. (1 John 5:10)

That's a pretty heavy charge to make, but it's time someone said it. The stakes are too high to keep ignoring the problem about not taking the Prophets seriously.

The message of the Prophets

This means, then, that the Biblical Prophets were witnesses of God, and what they testify about is important for us. They didn't just predict the future, and confront us with God's Word. It's *what they saw* that's important. If you check the messages of all the Prophets, you will find this constant theme in them all:

A prophet announced the coming kingdom of God.

We can best understand this if we use an example of early warfare. When two nations went to war against each other, the armies would move out into the field to fight each other – and then stop. Each side would send an emissary out to meet in the middle of the field. They would trade insults, show contempt for each other, and warn each other to give up or else. Then if they didn't manage to frighten the other side into submission, they would go back to their ranks and the fight would commence.

This is exactly what is happening with the Prophets. The Kingdom of God is coming to make war upon the kingdoms of the earth, to destroy the works of the devil, and set up a new kingdom with Christ as the King. And the Prophets are God's special messengers, sent to warn us – who are rebels on the enemy's side – that he is coming. The message is that we must give up now – repent

– before he gets here, because he will show no mercy on the wicked on the Day of Judgment. The day of mercy is *now*.

This is what the Prophets saw. They didn't just see God in Heaven, and report to us on how he's doing. The Lord was angry at the rebellion, wickedness, ignorance, and death in his world. He first formed Israel into a nation to rescue them from sin, and to give them the blessings of the covenant that he made with their father Abraham. He separated them from the nations, gave them their own land, gave them the Temple and the sacrificial system. They had everything they could ever want! Yet they continually rebelled against God; they exchanged the worship of God for idols, and learned the practices of their pagan neighbors. They thought the treasures of Heaven were of so little worth that they were willing to throw it all away for the pleasures of sin. So, God sent prophet after prophet with warnings: **repent**, before I come and destroy you.

> You are destroyed, O Israel, because you are against me, against your helper. (Hosea 13:9)

> I will bring you into the desert of the nations and there, face to face, I will execute judgment upon you. As I judged your fathers in the desert of the land of Egypt, so I will judge you, declares the Sovereign LORD. (Ezekiel 20:35)

> Your warriors, O Teman, will be terrified, and everyone in Esau's mountains will be cut down in the slaughter. Because of the violence against your brother Jacob, you will be covered with shame; you will be destroyed forever. (Obadiah 9-10)

Not only did the Prophets see the coming destruction, they saw the new kingdom that God would set up. This kingdom would be filled with holiness, righteousness and peace. God himself would rule this kingdom. In one of the most famous prophetic passages of the Old Testament we get a description of the kind of kingdom that God has in mind for those later days:

For to us a child is born, to us a son is given, and the government will be on his shoulders. And he will be called Wonderful Counselor, Mighty God, Everlasting Father, Prince of Peace. Of the increase of his government and peace there will be no end. He will reign on David's throne and over his kingdom, establishing and upholding it with justice and righteousness from that time on and forever. The zeal of the LORD Almighty will accomplish this. (Isaiah 9:6-7)

The point is that the Prophets *saw* all this. They were *eyewitnesses* of coming events: the shakeup of this world in its rebellion against God, and the restoration of what God had in mind when he first set up his kingdom on earth. How is it that they were able to see things in Heaven, and events that were still in the future? Peter tells us: the Holy Spirit (remember, he's the primary eyewitness of God's works) showed them. They were lifted up from earth and saw visions, they saw the kingdom of Heaven where God rules and all creatures serve him. They watched as God prepared his army, listened to his battle plans, and observed the Son of Man as he prepared for his coming as the Messiah.

What did the Prophets see?

If we understand the fact that the Prophets saw the destruction of this world's kingdoms, and the setting up of God's perfect Kingdom, the prophecies make much more sense than if we just look for predictions of the future. As an example, let's follow one prophet's message – Isaiah – and learn what it is that he saw.

- **What's wrong with this world:** The reason that God has plans to destroy this world that we live in is because it's so far off from his original Creation. God didn't originally make the world to be filled with sin and death; man did that to Creation.

The world is under the dominion of Satan now. Man let him in the door in the first place, by listening to his lies instead of obeying God's truth. And once the new master assumed control over his gullible and pitiful subjects, it was only natural that the devil's schemes would result in the opposite of what God wanted to happen in Creation.

Now the world is filled with the opposite of life and peace. We have sin all over the world, in everyone's heart, so deep-rooted that most people don't even know how much they offend their Creator with their lives. There is rebellion everywhere: nobody wants to do things God's ways even when they know what those ways are. They would rather live their lives in their own way and die! Darkness covers the earth; lies and deceit hide reality from us, and anybody who believes the devil's lies (which are always sugar-coated so that nobody really realizes that they are lies) will eventually be destroyed by following what isn't true. If you can get people to believe a lie, you can pretty much lead them into any kind of mischief you want them to commit. How many times have we seen that in the course of human events!

Our world can be described in three ways: *first*, it's full of sin, rebellion and corruption. Man has turned his back on God his Creator and Ruler, he refuses to obey God's perfect Law, and he has set up his own set of rules to live by that he thinks will satisfy his lusts and desires much better than will God's providence. *Second*, man has turned to false gods and worshipped them. He doesn't like what he has seen of the true God, and he prefers to bow down to a god that will cater to his desires. The thought of turning one's whole life over to a holy God is more than man can bear! *Third*, all of this leads to certain death. Rebels can't last long in God's creation. Though we think we can get away with our sin, we're foolish to think that; God won't allow the wicked to survive in his presence.

And that accounts for the sickness, misery, pain, destruction, and death that fills our world now. We can't seem to understand that there will be swift and certain retribution for sin.

The world is full of sickness, destruction and death. There are, of course, always efforts to alleviate human misery, but the causes of that misery are always with us and always tearing down the hard work we do to fix things. War, famine, disease, accidents, poverty – these have always been the rule in human history, not the exception. It's certainly not the world that God intended from the beginning. But it's the certain result of sin, which must always end in pain, misery and death. There's no escaping it in this world.

Man has become too attached to this world, and for some perverted reason he loves it. Even when he's been warned that the world will be destroyed, and those who value their souls had better give it up and seek a more permanent kingdom, man won't give up his sin and rebellion. He would rather defy God to his face and hold to his sin – and therefore die – instead of repent and live.

The Prophets saw this amazing state of affairs very clearly. They weren't put off by the moral façade that people put up to hide their hearts. Actually you can stroll down almost any modern street in today's society and see the same hypocrisy. People are "buying and selling, marrying and giving in marriage" as if nothing is wrong, as if life has always gone on in this way and always will. To us, it's just ordinary life. What they're hiding behind that false sense of security and pleasure, however, is a heart greedy for wickedness and rebellion. God sees an ignorant, heartless, selfish, godless, immoral culture that has not only failed to follow its original responsibilities from Creation, but they're absolutely worthless for the coming Kingdom. The Prophets saw all this, though.

Hear, O heavens! Listen, O earth! For the LORD has spoken: "I reared children and brought them up, but they have rebelled against me. The ox knows his master, the donkey his owner's manger, but Israel does not know, my people do not understand." Ah, sinful nation, a people loaded with guilt, a brood of evildoers, children given to corruption! They have forsaken the LORD; they have spurned the Holy One of Israel and turned their backs on him. Why should you be beaten anymore? Why do you persist in rebellion? Your whole head is injured, your whole heart afflicted. From the sole of your foot to the top of your head there is no soundness – only wounds and welts and open sores, not cleansed or bandaged or soothed with oil. Your country is desolate, your cities burned with fire; your fields are being stripped by foreigners right before you, laid waste as when overthrown by strangers. The Daughter of Zion is left like a shelter in a vineyard, like a hut in a field of melons, like a city under siege. Unless the LORD Almighty had left us some survivors, we would have become like Sodom, we would have been like Gomorrah. (Isaiah 2-9)

- **The King is coming:** The are scores of prophecies about Christ that most people in the Church know about. There are hundreds of them scattered through the Old Testament Prophets. They foretold what kind of person he would be, the works he would do, the treatment he would receive from men, the goals he had in mind in coming here, the results of his work on the nation of Israel and on the whole world. All of his ministry is so well described in the Prophets that there is little left to the imagination.

Sometimes, however, what we think we already know has more depth to it than we realize. For example, it's obvious that the Jews completely missed the whole point of the prophecies of Christ, because "he came to that which was his own, but *his own did not receive him*." (John 1:11) Jesus came to claim his kingdom among the Jews, but they didn't know (in spite of the fact that their Bibles carefully described it beforehand!) that Christ is King of the *heart*. He came to rule a *spiritual* kingdom, not the physical nation of the Jews. If they had paid attention to the Prophets, they would have known the kind of spiritual ministry and Kingdom that Jesus had in mind.

For example, the Prophets focused on what really bothered the Lord about the Israelites. They described the sinful nature of the human heart; and they outlined the sacrifice that must be made to atone for our sins.

> I will give you a new heart and put a new spirit in you; I will remove from you your heart of stone and give you a heart of flesh. And I will put my Spirit in you and move you to follow my decrees and be careful to keep my laws. You will live in the land I gave your forefathers; you will be my people, and I will be your God. I will save you from all your uncleanness. (Ezekiel 36:26-29)

That's the ministry of Jesus, in a nutshell. In fact, the Prophets described his ministry so accurately and completely that he himself said:

> You diligently study the Scriptures because you think that by them you possess eternal life. These are the Scriptures that testify about me, yet you refuse to come to me to have life. (John 5:39-40)

The Prophets realized that when Jesus came, he wouldn't just stay to fix our problems and then leave again forever. They knew he was coming to set up an *eternal kingdom* over us. He's going to solve our problem of *sin* for good.

> You shall call his name Jesus, for he shall save his people from their sin. (Matthew 1:21)

Sin means, basically, rebellion against God's Law. "Everyone who sins breaks the law; in fact, sin is lawlessness." (1 John 3:4) As we saw above in Isaiah 9 and Ezekiel 36, Jesus' main concern is that we start doing what God requires of us for a change. He will assume the throne over us and rule us (in love and mercy, to be sure, because he wants to change us into his image and live with him forever); but this time everyone *will* conform to the Law of God. He himself is going to change us so that we will obey him with all of our hearts. Then we really will be saved; it won't be dependent on our efforts (because we always fail when we try it on our own will and strength) but on Christ's work that can't fail.

There's something else in the Prophets about Christ that we mustn't miss. The Lord used King David to set up the kingdom of Israel along certain lines. God raised up David as a "man after God's own heart" (1 Samuel 13:14) – which means that David did things the way that God wanted them to be done. The King of Israel must rule God's people a certain way, and achieve certain results in order to fulfill God's will for their lives.

David was a pattern for all the kings to follow: each son who ascended the throne of Israel was compared to his father David.

> So Solomon did evil in the eyes of the LORD; he did not follow the LORD completely, as David his father had done.

Asa did what was right in the eyes of
the LORD, as his father David had done.

This is because God laid down the pattern, the rules, in David's reign. In order to continue to please God, *all* of David's successors had to do the same kind of work among the people of God.

Jesus was the son of David, which the Gospels make a lot of. But the Prophets also focused on his royal lineage. The reason, of course, is that Jesus must build the Kingdom of God in the same way that his father David had done! The new Kingdom would run on the same divine principles as the old one. This should help us understand the "why" behind many of the things that Jesus did in his ministry; we can go back to the Prophets for the explanation of how Jesus' work is tied back to the original kingdom under David.

Paul said that one should study the Prophets, because it's *there* that we will learn about Christ and be saved through knowledge of him! He called the Old Testament, which is mainly the book of the Prophets –

> ... the holy Scriptures, which are able to make you *wise for salvation through faith in Christ Jesus.* (2 Timothy 3:15)

And in this Old Testament we read in one of the Prophets about the Son of David and how he will build a new kingdom on earth:

> A shoot will come up from the stump of Jesse; from his roots a Branch will bear fruit. The Spirit of the LORD will rest on him– the Spirit of wisdom and of understanding, the Spirit of counsel and of power, the Spirit of knowledge and of the fear of the LORD – and he will delight in the fear of the LORD. He

will not judge by what he sees with his eyes, or decide by what he hears with his ears; but with righteousness he will judge the needy, with justice he will give decisions for the poor of the earth. He will strike the earth with the rod of his mouth; with the breath of his lips he will slay the wicked. Righteousness will be his belt and faithfulness the sash around his waist. (Isaiah 11:1-5)

- **The people of the kingdom:** It would be a shame to tear down this world of sinners, build a perfect kingdom in its place, and then have leftover sinners around to ruin things all over again. The Lord isn't stupid. He refuses to let sinners into his new kingdom. The Kingdom of God will be filled with the righteous, but no sinners. *There is going to be an end to sin.* The Prophets knew that: they saw who would be allowed into God's Kingdom. Though their testimony may have discouraged their hearers at first – only the perfect would be citizens of the kingdom, they said – there was actually a ray of hope in their message too.

The wicked had *no* hope, according to the Prophets.

> I will purge you of those who revolt and rebel against me. Although I will bring them out of the land where they are living, yet they will not enter the land of Israel. Then you will know that I am the LORD. (Ezekiel 20:38)

The righteous, however, will be welcomed into the kingdom:

> No lion will be there, nor will any ferocious beast get up on it; they will not be found there. But only the redeemed will walk there, and the ransomed of the LORD will return. They will enter Zion with singing; everlasting joy will

crown their heads. Gladness and joy will overtake them, and sorrow and sighing will flee away. (Isaiah 35:9-10)

Remember, there are walls around Jerusalem; they are designed to keep the enemy *out*. But notice carefully who will be let in: not those who *make themselves* righteous, but the *redeemed* and the *ransomed* – in other words, those whom the Lord has called, justified, sanctified, and glorified. There is a great deal of difference! Those who try to make themselves holy and acceptable to God will fail; nobody can keep the Law perfectly (and it *must* be kept perfectly or, on the basis of a single sin, we will be judged lawbreakers – "For whoever keeps the whole Law and yet stumbles at just one point is guilty of breaking all of it." James 2:10). But those who look to Christ to save them from their sin and redeem them from this world of darkness will be given new hearts, the righteousness of Christ, faith, spiritual power, encouragement, and the hope of Heaven.

And everyone who calls on the name of the LORD will be saved; for on Mount Zion and in Jerusalem there will be deliverance, as the LORD has said, among the survivors whom the LORD calls. (Joel 2:32)

The wolf will live with the lamb, the leopard will lie down with the goat, the calf and the lion and the yearling together; and a little child will lead them. The cow will feed with the bear, their young will lie down together, and the lion will eat straw like the ox. The infant will play near the hole of the cobra, and the young child put his hand into the viper's nest. They will neither harm nor destroy on all my holy mountain, for the earth will be full of the knowledge of the LORD as the waters cover the sea. (Isaiah 11:6-9)

- **What it will be like to live in that kingdom:** Imagine a place where there is light and life so full that darkness and death is no longer possible. Imagine a place where all the people who live there love each other, they live in peaceful harmony, and they live only to do each other good. Imagine a place where God rules over all, and he provides – as only a good King will – for all the needs of all of his people, so that there is never any unfulfilled need. This is utopia, isn't it?

We can imagine and hope for such a place, but the Prophets *saw* it. And their testimony isn't their imaginations or hopes; they "saw them and welcomed them from a distance." (Hebrews 11:13) For example, this is what the prophet Isaiah saw:

> Behold, I will create new heavens and a new earth. The former things will not be remembered, nor will they come to mind. But be glad and rejoice forever in what I will create, for I will create Jerusalem to be a delight and its people a joy. I will rejoice over Jerusalem and take delight in my people; the sound of weeping and of crying will be heard in it no more ... Before they call I will answer; while they are still speaking I will hear. The wolf and the lamb will feed together, and the lion will eat straw like the ox, but dust will be the serpent's food. They will neither harm nor destroy on all my holy mountain, says the LORD. (Isaiah 65:17-19,24-25)

Joel saw the Spirit poured out on all flesh. Hosea saw the Lord bring his people to him as a husband draws his wife close to him. Ezekiel saw the Glory of the Lord return to dwell among his people. Daniel saw the Ancient of Days ruling over all nations. Amos saw the people of God brought back from exile, planting their vineyards, never to be uprooted again. Micah saw the nations coming to Jerusalem, and putting away all weapons of war. Zechariah saw the Lord as king over the whole earth.

The King who comes to set up his Kingdom on earth has a mandate from Heaven. When God first created the world, he made it very good – in other words, it was exactly what he wanted it to be. It was in perfect balance, and every creature supported every other creature in order to achieve the effect that God wanted. The world couldn't have been made better than it was. Sin, of course, upset the balance of Creation. So when the King comes, he's going to restore the perfect balance that the Creator originally had in mind – though not in the same way. Now, instead of making a physical world, he's going to build a spiritual Kingdom. But it will have the same characteristics of the first one: it will be a perfect world where men rule under God, and they will enjoy the blessings that God gives them in that new world. Man will be responsible under God to carry out his duties – which will be spiritual duties designed to glorify God. So that new world will return to the original idea of Genesis 1, but this time it will be spiritual, eternal, and not susceptible to failure or decay this time. The Creator intends to make a new world that he will call "very good."

- **What will happen to this world:** Remember that the Lord threatened to destroy this world. He isn't simply going to set up a Heaven far away somewhere and take us to live there – all the while leaving this world in its darkness and wickedness. This world that we live in now is a kingdom: it's ruled by "the ruler of the kingdom of the air, the spirit who is now at work in those who are disobedient." (Ephesians 2:2) God will not tolerate this world any more; he will not let a challenge to his authority and holiness continue to exist. Therefore, it must be eliminated.

You must understand that when God does something, he does it to get glory. That means that he wants those watching to know that he deserves credit for being who he is. We don't often give him credit for things – though he says that he rules over the nations, we don't fear him; though he says that only he is holy, we think that our holiness will impress him; though he says that he wants to save sinners from their sins, we don't want saving. In fact, God gets almost no glory from the world as it stands now.

When he comes in judgment, however, he intends to make up for all the glory he didn't get in history. The Prophets knew what he was after. In rebuking the nations, he intends to correct the false notions that people have had about him. They will not miss the lesson this time!

> But this is what the LORD says: "Yes, captives will be taken from warriors, and plunder retrieved from the fierce; I will contend with those who contend with you, and your children I will save. I will make your oppressors eat their own flesh; they will be drunk on their own blood, as with wine. *Then all mankind will know that I, the LORD, am your Savior, your Redeemer, the Mighty One of Jacob.*" (Isaiah 49:25-26)

This is just one of many prophecies about what will happen when the Lord comes. He will punish sinners with death; *then* men will know that he was serious when he demanded obedience from them. He will destroy the nations; *then* men will know that he really is the King of kings. He will reverse the hurt and damage that the wicked inflicted on the righteous; *then* men will know that the Father protects his little ones and inflicts his wrath against those who dare to touch them. He will destroy all wealth and everything that men hold precious; *then* he will show his utter contempt for treasures of this world, and everything that doesn't do our souls eternal good.

You see, there is nothing here, in this old world, that he can use in his new kingdom. The Prophets often use images and symbols to describe what God's coming kingdom will be like – it often sounds like a paradise on earth, to read their account – but actually the reality is beyond the normal words of man to describe. They struggled with the same problem we do: we don't have the words to describe what Heaven will be like, only shadows and vague ideas about spiritual realities. But, as Hebrews testifies, the Prophets were looking past this world to the new one to come:

> Instead, they were longing for a better country – a heavenly one. Therefore God is not ashamed to be called their God, for he has prepared a city for them. (Hebrews 11:16)

> See, the LORD is going to lay waste the earth and devastate it; he will ruin its face and scatter its inhabitants – it will be the same for priest as for people, for master as for servant, for mistress as for maid, for seller as for buyer, for borrower as for lender, for debtor as for creditor. The earth will be completely laid waste and totally plundered. The LORD has spoken this word. The earth dries up and withers, the world languishes and withers, the exalted of the earth languish. The earth is defiled by its people; they have disobeyed the laws, violated the statutes and broken the everlasting covenant. Therefore a curse consumes the earth; its people must bear their guilt. Therefore earth's inhabitants are burned up, and very few are left. The new wine dries up and the vine withers; all the merrymakers groan. The gaiety of the

tambourines is stilled, the noise of the revelers has stopped, the joyful harp is silent. No longer do they drink wine with a song; the beer is bitter to its drinkers. The ruined city lies desolate; the entrance to every house is barred. In the streets they cry out for wine; all joy turns to gloom, all gaiety is banished from the earth. The city is left in ruins, its gate is battered to pieces. So will it be on the earth and among the nations, as when an olive tree is beaten, or as when gleanings are left after the grape harvest. (Isaiah 24:1-13)

The greatest of the Prophets

You may be surprised to learn who the greatest prophet of the Old Testament was. We don't have to guess; we are told in Deuteronomy who he was:

Since then, no prophet has risen in Israel like Moses, whom the LORD knew face to face, who did all those miraculous signs and wonders the LORD sent him to do in Egypt – to Pharaoh and to all his officials and to his whole land. For no one has ever shown the mighty power or performed the awesome deeds that Moses did in the sight of all Israel. (Deuteronomy 34:10-12)

There is a reason for this. When God called the Israelites out of Egypt, out of the slavery they were under, they became a new nation. Moses became the leader of the infant nation of Israel (we aren't counting Abraham, the father of the Israelites, because the nation didn't really come together until Moses' day). There was an enormous job to be done: the Law had to be given and enforced, the Tabernacle had to be built, the sacrifices outlined and started, the priests to train, the civil laws to lay out. Then when Israel started out into the wilderness, Moses had to lead them in the right direction, pray for food and water for the millions in the company, pronounce God's wrath against sinners and blessings on those who obeyed, judge cases of law between accused and accuser, lead the people into battle against their enemies, interpret God's mysterious actions to the people, and many more great and small details that go into making a new nation from scratch. Plus, all this had to be done so well that the system that he set up would last for countless generations into the future – millions of descendants who would all depend on this work of Moses in the beginning. It was a job that would make any sensible man humble at the thought.

So, in order to pull all of this off, God appeared to Moses in a special way:

> When a prophet of the LORD is among you, I reveal myself to him in visions, I speak to him in dreams. But this is not true of my servant Moses; he is faithful in all my house. *With him I speak face to face*, clearly and not in riddles; *he sees the form of the LORD.* (Numbers 12:6-8)

Moses saw God, and the kingdom of God, so clearly that he was enabled to build God's kingdom on earth in full knowledge and confidence. God showed him every detail, so perfectly that future generations could also have confidence in the fact that, if they followed the Mosaic Law to the letter, then they would please God too.

For example, when it came time to build the Tabernacle, it was absolutely critical that they get every detail correct; their salvation depended on its accuracy! God is holy, and he expects anyone who approaches him, for any reason, to do it in the prescribed manner, and with the correct ceremony. He will not accept false worship – that is, worship that he didn't command himself. So Moses and his helpers were filled with the Spirit and shown the Temple which is in Heaven; and that, then, became their pattern for the Tabernacle on earth:

> They serve at a sanctuary that is a copy and shadow of what is in Heaven. This is why Moses was warned when he was about to build the tabernacle: "See to it that you make everything according to the pattern *shown you* on the mountain." (Hebrews 8:5)

The point is that Moses witnessed the Heavenly Temple, and testified to Israel of what he saw when he built the earthly Tabernacle. None of it was his own invention. He was an eyewitness of the world of God.

The rest of the Prophets of Israel – Elijah, Elisha, Isaiah, Jeremiah, Daniel and the rest – were actually the "support group" for the Mosaic Law. They of course didn't make themselves prophets; our original definition of a prophet holds true of all of them. God called them to go to Israel and rebuke the people for straying away from the kingdom that Moses first laid out for them. The message was always the same: repent, go back to the Law of Moses, go back to your God that you first met at Mt. Sinai, return to the covenant of your fathers. If you do not repent, then God will come and destroy you and set up a new kingdom, one in which he *will* reign over a *holy* people as he intended from the beginning.

Rejecting the Prophets

There's an interesting aspect of the ministry of the Prophets that was true from the very first one, Moses, all the way through the rest of them: their message was often rejected. Persecution of prophets is proverbial. By Jesus' time, the treatment that the prophets of the Old Testament received from the people they ministered to was well known:

> Blessed are you when people insult you, persecute you and falsely say all kinds of evil against you because of me. Rejoice and be glad, because great is your reward in heaven, for in the same way they persecuted the prophets who were before you. (Matthew 5:11-12)

Basically, the people didn't believe the Prophets' testimony. The prophet claimed to have seen God's world, and *that* – his eyewitness testimony – is what people didn't accept. For example, when Micaiah the prophet told the king Ahab of a scene he witnessed in Heaven (one which foretold that Ahab's other false prophets would lead him into a defeat in battle), he was challenged by someone who didn't believe that Micaiah had really seen such a thing:

Then Zedekiah son of Kenaanah went up and slapped Micaiah in the face. "Which way did the spirit from the LORD go when he went from me to speak to you?" he asked. (1 Kings 22:24)

But Zedekiah was wrong. Micaiah really had seen what he testified to, and events turned out just as he had predicted. Furthermore, the Lord evidently had a special punishment in mind for Zedekiah himself because he refused to believe the prophet's testimony: "Micaiah replied, 'You will find out on the day you go to hide in an inner room.'" (1 Kings 22:25)

Daniel was thrown to the lions; Jeremiah was thrown into a well; Jezebel threatened death to Elijah if she could ever catch him; Ahab sent a small army after Elisha; even Moses was challenged by Korah and other leaders of the Israelites, including his own brother and sister, Aaron and Miriam. Prophets always ran the risk of offending the ones they spoke to, mainly because the people didn't want to hear of a King coming to rule over them.

You snakes! You brood of vipers! How will you escape being condemned to hell? Therefore I am sending you prophets and wise men and teachers. Some of them you will kill and crucify; others you will flog in your synagogues and pursue from town to town. And so upon you will come all the righteous blood that has been shed on earth, from the blood of righteous Abel to the blood of Zechariah son of Berekiah, whom you murdered between the temple and the altar. I tell you the truth, all this will come upon this generation. (Matthew 23:33-36)

But how dependable are the Prophets? Jesus told us that the testimony of the Prophets is crucial for our understanding of the Kingdom of God. In his story of the rich man and Lazarus, when the rich man pleaded with Abraham to send someone to his family with news of what Hell is like, Abraham refused. He said that the man's family already had an eyewitness account of Heaven and Hell, so they already knew what to do in order to avoid the one and make sure of the other. In fact, this testimony of the Prophets is more reliable than if someone would miraculously rise from the dead and appear to us!

> He answered, 'Then I beg you, father, send Lazarus to my father's house, for I have five brothers. Let him warn them, so that they will not also come to this place of torment.' Abraham replied, They have Moses and the Prophets; let them listen to them.' 'No, father Abraham,' he said, 'but if someone from the dead goes to them, they will repent.' 'He said to him, 'If they do not listen to Moses and the Prophets, they will not be convinced even if someone rises from the dead.' (Luke 16:27-31)

Summary

Basically, the Old Testament Prophets were eyewitnesses to the reality of God. It's a *legal* document: it consists of eyewitness accounts of people who saw God at work among the Israelites. They know that it was God; they saw *him* in the events that took place. Modern skeptics doubt their testimony, but they have no good reason for doubting people who said that they saw and heard God. Unless they were all liars (and who can justifiably call them that?), our only option is to believe their claims. They testified to the fact that the holy God is coming to punish the wicked and reward the righteous; will he find faith on the earth when he comes?

> Therefore, since we are surrounded by such a great cloud of witnesses, let us throw off everything that hinders and the sin that so easily entangles, and let us run with perseverance the race marked out for us. (Hebrews 12:1)

The Witness of the Father

The incarnation of the Son of God was such an important event in human history that it had to be witnessed. We've already looked at the fact that the Apostles and Prophets all knew the truth about Jesus, and revealed facts about him that we wouldn't have otherwise known or figured out on our own. And the Spirit of God constantly testifies to the Christ so that we who have come after him in history can personally know him.

But there's another witness of Christ, another point of view that we haven't yet looked at – and he's probably the most important witness of all. The Father gave his own testimony about his Son that proved to be an overwhelming confirmation of the true nature of Christ.

The Father's purpose in testifying about Jesus is twofold:

First, he wants to prove to us that Jesus is what he claims to be. Remember that Jesus set aside his glory before coming to earth. He used to sit with God the Father on the throne of Heaven, and he shared God's glory from before time began. The angels fell at his feet and worshipped him. But when he was born to a carpenter's wife in poverty and obscurity, the world not only didn't know what had happened, they rejected him when they were told about him – even though he's their rightful king. There just wasn't anything about him that would have convinced them that he was the King of kings and rightful ruler over all people and nations.

But Jesus insisted on keeping a low profile. He preached the Gospel all through Israel, and he did miracles to help the poor and needy; but he refused to act like a king in the way that his friends wanted him to. If he was going to get any credibility with the world to back up his claims, someone else would have to do it – he just wouldn't.

That's exactly what the Father was interested in. Jesus never lifted himself up. He let the Father glorify him in the time and place he chose to. And God the Father did many things in the ministry of Christ to confirm that, yes, Jesus *really is* what he claims to be. As Jesus worked, the Father gave him power and success at every step. Jesus knew very well where the power for his ministry was coming from, because we see him thanking his Father on various occasions. We also see him praying for what he needed on a daily basis. The foundation of Jesus' life-work was the Father; Jesus "did nothing on his own." (John 8:28)

Second, the Father proved to Jesus' followers that he really was the Son of God. Only a divine being would be able to do the things that Jesus did. Even the Prophets of the Old Testament didn't do the kinds of miracles that the disciples witnessed. At one point Jesus asked his disciples who they thought he was. Based on what they saw, Peter answered:

> You are the Christ, the Son of the living God.
> (Matthew 16:16)

And Jesus told Peter that he could only have seen that if the Father had revealed it to him. The Father's business is to make sure we don't miss the point: Jesus is God come into the flesh. As John says elsewhere –

> This is how you can recognize the Spirit of God: Every spirit that acknowledges that Jesus Christ has come in the flesh is from God, but every spirit that does not acknowledge Jesus is not from God. (1 John 4:2-3)

The reason we need to know this about Jesus is so that, first of all, we will learn to worship him as the God of Israel; we can trust him with the very issues that we would turn to God for in the first place. Secondly, we need to understand that Jesus isn't a different God (as so many people accuse the Christians of). He is Israel's God, the God who led the Israelites out of Egypt and into the Promised Land. He has the same characteristics, the same personality, the same ways and goals, as the God they've been accustomed to in the Old Testament.

And we must remember the function of an eyewitness, because the same applies to the Father when he revealed the truth to us about his Son. He affirms to us, the jury, that he *saw* the reality of God in Christ. He testifies that what we've heard about Christ is absolutely true, because he was there at the beginning with him. His testimony is iron-clad proof that Jesus really is the Son of God, and that in him are all the things that we need spiritually. And the particular way that the Father testifies to us about Jesus makes his argument all the more convincing.

Supporting the work of Christ

One reason that Jesus came in such humble circumstances (among many!) was to be the pattern for all of God's people. In other words, he is in himself the example of how we all ought to live. Unfortunately many people agree with this statement for the wrong reason. They think that they can live as Jesus did: doing good deeds, living a moral life, and so on. What they don't realize is that the secret to Jesus' life and ministry is the Spirit of God. The Spirit filled Jesus with power from on high to do the *impossible*, what can't be done by mere man on his own. So those who think that they can live like Jesus lived, and do it without the power and wisdom of the Spirit, will find themselves unaccountably failing in their misguided zeal.

Jesus tapped the power of Heaven in order to do what he did. He relied on this principle, because it's the method that all of God's children must use if they hope to live by faith. And God the Father honored his faith by granting his requests. That's the testimony that the Father made about his Son: he was pleased with Jesus, and he provided Jesus with everything he needed. We need no stronger testimony about what the Father thought about Christ than answered prayers and a successful ministry.

- **Answering Christ's prayers** – On several occasions we find Jesus praying to the Father. This of all his activities shows how much he depended on his Father for everything. It's humbling to see the Son of God on his knees, imploring for answers from the Throne of Grace – and to know how little we, who have far more reason to beg for God's help, actually turn to him!

Jesus prayed fervently for the things he needed in his life and ministry. His were not ceremonial prayers, but urgent pleadings for real needs.

> During the days of Jesus' life on earth, he offered up prayers and petitions with loud cries and tears to the one who could save him from death, and he was heard because of his reverent submission. Although he was a son, he learned obedience from what he suffered and, once made perfect, he became the source of eternal salvation for all who obey him and was designated by God to be high priest in the order of Melchizedek. (Hebrews 5:7-10)

> On reaching the place, he said to them, "Pray that you will not fall into temptation." He withdrew about a stone's throw beyond them, knelt down and prayed, "Father, if you are willing, take this cup from me; yet not my will, but yours be done." An angel from heaven appeared to him and strengthened him. And being in anguish, he prayed more earnestly, and his sweat was like drops of blood falling to the ground. (Luke 22:40-44)

He evidently expected real results; he saw the treasures in Heaven that he needed and wasn't going to be satisfied until the Father gave them to him. Again, we have to contrast that approach of faith and confidence and urgency with our own prayer time, which is usually a ceremonial exercise. We are so used to getting *no* answers that we usually ask without any real hope of getting anything.

The Father loved his Son, especially because Jesus was so well fitted for the job ahead of him. Whenever the Son asked for something from God, therefore, he knew that his Father would always hear and answer. He knew his Father's heart:

> This is my Son, whom I love; with him I am well pleased. (Matthew 3:17)

> He was heard because of his reverent submission. (Hebrews 5:7)

> Father, I thank you that you have heard me. I knew that you always hear me, but I said this for the benefit of the people standing here, that they may believe that you sent me. (John 11:41)

When the disciples saw Jesus' prayers consistently answered, they of course wanted to learn his secret. They came to him once and asked him how to pray in a way that they would get answers:

> When he finished, one of his disciples said to him, "Lord, teach us to pray, just as John taught his disciples." (Luke 11:1)

And when Jesus told them, as he did once to Peter, that he had prayed for them, they no doubt felt assured that the Father would answer that prayer because of Christ's special influence with the Father:

> Simon, Simon, Satan has asked to sift you as wheat. But I have prayed for you, Simon, that your faith may not fail. (Luke 22:31)

Prayer, then, was the starting point of Christ's ministry. He asked for what he needed, therefore the Father gave it to him. He followed his own advice about asking in faith and expecting the kind of answers that we really need from Heaven:

> Ask and it will be given to you; seek and you will find; knock and the door will be opened to you. For everyone who asks receives; he who seeks finds; and to him who knocks, the door will be opened. "Which of you, if his son asks for bread, will give him a stone? Or if he asks for a fish, will give him a snake? If you, then, though you are evil, know how to give good gifts to your children, how much more will your Father in heaven give good gifts to those who ask him! (Matthew 7:7-11)

And this was what honored God the most – prayers of faith, asking for the resources of Heaven to tackle earth's problems. It was the occasion for God to manifest his love for his Son, and provided a platform to start building the Kingdom of God over which his Son would rule.

- **Miracles** – Miracles were an important part of Jesus' ministry, more important perhaps than you might realize. Many skeptics of our day doubt that such things really happened. Our scientific sophistication has pretty much talked us out of the possibility of miracles – as if those people in those days were too naïve to realize when they were witnessing a scientific principle of the world's workings, instead of a miracle.

But as we've already seen, miracles really did happen in Jesus' ministry. The disciples were not fools. They saw impossible things happen under Jesus' hands. If we were there, we would be just as dumbfounded about them, notwithstanding our scientific expertise. We are forced to accept their eyewitness testimony about what they saw.

But the reason that the miracles happened in the first place was that God made them happen. *Only God can do miracles.* We can be sure, when we witness a miracle, that

God is there doing his special work. Miracles are impossible, and we know that God can do the impossible:

> With man this is impossible, but with God all things are possible. (Matthew 19:26)

> For nothing is impossible with God. (Luke 1:37)

Jesus had great need of miracles in his ministry, because so many people he met were in desperate straits. They were sick, lonely, hungry, ignorant, lost, and some even dead. In order to fix the condition that they were in, Jesus had to do the impossible. But – as he always insisted – he would *not* do this on his own. One of his missions was to display the power of God: he looked to the Father to do the miracles through him.

God the Father answered his prayers by doing miracles through the ministry of Christ, whenever he asked and wherever he needed them. But in doing those miracles, he was showing the other people watching Jesus who this amazing man really is. God testified to the special relationship between them by doing what others couldn't do.

> We must pay more careful attention, therefore, to what we have heard, so that we do not drift away. For if the message spoken by angels was binding, and every violation and disobedience received its just punishment, how shall we escape if we ignore such a great salvation? This salvation, which was first announced by the Lord, was confirmed to us by those who heard him. God also testified to it by signs, wonders and various miracles, and gifts of the Holy Spirit distributed according to his will. (Hebrews 2:1-4)

> We know that God does not listen to sinners. He listens to the godly man who does his will. (John 9:31)

When John heard in prison what Christ was doing, he sent his disciples to ask him, "Are you the one who was to come, or should we expect someone else?" Jesus replied, "Go back and report to John what you hear and see: The blind receive sight, the lame walk, those who have leprosy are cured, the deaf hear, the dead are raised, and the good news is preached to the poor. Blessed is the man who does not fall away on account of me." (Matthew 11:2-6)

Do not believe me unless I do what my Father does. But if I do it, even though you do not believe me, believe the miracles, that you may know and understand that the Father is in me, and I in the Father. (John 10:37-38)

In other words, the miracles themselves were proof that this was the Son of God come in the flesh. God – Immanuel – had come to set up his eternal Kingdom. The Jews should have recognized him immediately. The fact that they didn't shows that they didn't realize the vital importance of miracles. They should have known, from studying their Old Testament, that God builds his Kingdom through miracles, because natural means won't accomplish his eternal and spiritual goals. So when Jesus came doing the *same miracles*, building his Kingdom in the *same way* as the God of the Old Testament, this was proof (which would hold up in court) that it was the same God at work.

But if I drive out demons by the Spirit of God, then the kingdom of God has come upon you. (Matthew 12:28)

All the people were astonished and said, "Could this be the Son of David?" (Matthew 12:23)

- **Words given to Christ** – Another proof that God was behind everything that Jesus did is that Christ only spoke those things that his Father told him to say. This too is surprising to us, because we would have thought that Jesus, who is the Logos himself, the incarnate Word through whom the world was made in the beginning (John 1:1-3), would certainly have known what to say to people in his ministry. But true to form, he refused to do it on his own. He instead gave the credit to his Father for all that he said in his preaching and teaching:

> I have testimony weightier than that of John. For the very work that the Father has given me to finish, and which I am doing, testifies that the Father has sent me. (John 5:36)

> Don't you believe that I am in the Father, and that the Father is in me? The words I say to you are not just my own. Rather, it is the Father, living in me, who is doing his work. Believe me when I say that I am in the Father and the Father is in me; or at least believe on the evidence of the miracles themselves. (John 14:10)

> Everything that I learned from my Father I have made known to you. (John 15:15)

The reason, again, is that Jesus must say the same things that the God of the Old Testament said. It's the same God, preaching the same faith that Abraham himself learned. The Old Testament actually teaches the same God that the New Testament does; there aren't two Gods in the Bible. Most people get confused about the stories of God in the Old Testament when they try to match them with what they know of Jesus' teachings. For example, his teaching about the Law is really confusing, because it seems as though he's setting aside the Old Testament Law:

> You have heard that it was said to the people long ago, 'Do not murder, and anyone who murders will be subject to judgment.' But I tell you that anyone who is angry with his brother will be subject to judgment. (Matthew 5:21-22)

But his Father told him to say this. If you go back to the Old Testament you will see God say the same thing about this subject that Jesus taught:

> Do not hate your brother in your heart.
> (Leviticus 19:17)

This is important to see. The Old Testament is a very spiritual book. The Law was a stumbling block to the Jews, it's true, and the Christians have received a wonderful solution to fulfilling the Law without having themselves to follow the Law. But the message, and the goal, are always the same. Jesus only reinforced the Old Testament teachings in his ministry. If we think he contradicted it or set it aside, it's only because we don't understand the spiritual depth of the Old yet.

> Do not think that I have come to abolish the Law or the Prophets; I have not come to abolish them but to fulfill them. I tell you the truth, until heaven and earth disappear, not the smallest letter, not the least stroke of a pen, will by any means disappear from the Law until everything is accomplished. Anyone who breaks one of the least of these commandments and teaches others to do the same will be called least in the kingdom of heaven, but whoever practices and teaches these commands will be called great in the kingdom of heaven. For I tell you that unless your righteousness surpasses that of the Pharisees and the teachers of the law, you will certainly not enter the kingdom of heaven. (Matthew 5:17-20)

The disciples knew that what Jesus said to them were "words of life."

> Simon Peter answered him, "Lord, to whom shall we go? You have the words of eternal life. We believe and know that you are the Holy One of God." (John 6:68-69)

Whenever he taught them, the truth that he gave them set them free from the ignorance and bondage that the lies of the enemy burdened them with. He lifted their hearts up to the presence of God in what he said. This power behind his teaching was proof from God, given through the activity of the Spirit, that Jesus' words were from Heaven.

Jesus was also obligated to keep and fulfill the covenant made with Abraham. If you know what that covenant consisted of, you would know that everything that Jesus did and said was for the sole purpose of making sure that covenant was carried out among God's people. The spiritual blessings of the Gospel are the heart of that Abrahamic Covenant; if we get anything from God, it's only because of that. And Jesus knew how legally binding it was in the community of faith. He therefore would do nothing to jeopardize or compromise that legal agreement between God and his people. And as he kept God's side of the bargain, God honored his faithfulness by fulfilling the terms of the covenant for his people.

- **Work given to Christ** – Christ kept to the eternal plan that the Father had first originated at the beginning of the world. He came to do the Father's work, not his own:

> "My food," said Jesus, "is to do the will of him who sent me and to finish his work." (John 4:34)

> The words I say to you are not just my own. Rather, it is the Father, living in me, who is doing his work. (John 14:10)

And we can see in his ministry the blossoming of the Kingdom of God. It's as if Jesus put his spade in the earth, planted it with the Word, watered it with the Spirit, and what resulted was eternal fruit to please the Father – who is the owner of the garden.

> I will sing for the one I love a song about his vineyard: My loved one had a vineyard on a fertile

hillside. He dug it up and cleared it of stones and planted it with the choicest vines. He built a watchtower in it and cut out a winepress as well. Then he looked for a crop of good grapes, but it yielded only bad fruit …The vineyard of the LORD Almighty is the house of Israel, and the men of Judah are the garden of his delight. (Isaiah 5:1-2,7)

A farmer went out to sow his seed. (Matthew 13:3)

As Jesus did the Father's work, fruit resulted. God honored his work of faith because Jesus was faithful to the Father. Again we have the Father's confirmation, the Father's testimony, that *this is* the work that God wants done on the earth: he gave Jesus success in everything he set his hand to, because Jesus was doing the *right things*.

Paul tells us that Jesus came to build a Kingdom with the intention of someday turning over that Kingdom to the Father:

Then the end will come, when he hands over the kingdom to God the Father after he has destroyed all dominion, authority and power. For he must reign until he has put all his enemies under his feet. The last enemy to be destroyed is death. For he "has put everything under his feet." Now when it says that "everything" has been put under him, it is clear that this does not include God himself, who put everything under Christ. When he has done this, then the Son himself will be made subject to him who put everything under him, so that God may be all in all. (1 Corinthians 15:24-28)

When on Pentecost the Church was born, we received ample testimony to the fact that God does indeed want a Kingdom on earth. Not a physical one, but a spiritual Kingdom over which Jesus rules from the throne in Heaven. The growth and prosperity of the Church is God's answer to

Christ's initial "spade work" during his life and ministry here.

Revealing the Son of God

The birth of Christ completely surprised the Jews. They were expecting the Messiah at any moment, but they certainly didn't expect him to arrive like he did! They were hoping that he'd be born of more noble blood, in a great family, and that his rise to fame would be immediate and meteoric. But when Jesus was born to a poor carpenter's wife, surrounded by rumors of infidelity, and in a stable – that was too much for the Jews to accept. They pretty much ignored him and went on looking for another Messiah.

But as we've seen already, God had good reasons for introducing Jesus to the world in this strange way. Another reason that he did it was because he wants us to accept who Jesus is *by faith*, not by sight.

Our physical senses are undependable when it comes to learning about God. We've trained ourselves to rely on our senses so completely that we tend to judge the worth of something by what it looks like, or whether it appeals to one of our senses. But God is Spirit: we can't even know God with our physical senses. If we're to know anything about God, we have to gain a new skill that will enable us to reach out spiritually and find him.

That's what the Spirit does for us. He gives us the ability, the power, to wake up and know God in our souls – we can now be aware of God's presence. That's what the Scripture means by being "born again." (John 3:3) And whenever we want to get in touch with God, we have to do it through the Spirit who brings us spiritually into God's presence. Through him we can come up to God himself and present our requests to him. Through the Spirit we can know what it is that we want from God – we see it there, it's part of the treasures of Heaven that we're heir to – and reach out for it and take it.

And this is what the Bible means by "living by faith." (Romans 1:17) **Faith is living in the light of God's world.** We can see God, we can see him on his throne, we can see the spiritual riches in Christ that are ours for the asking. The eyes of our souls are opened and we *know* what we firmly believe in – by spiritual experience.

> Now faith is being sure of what we hope for and certain of what we do not see ... And without faith it is impossible to please God, because anyone who comes to him must believe that he exists and that he rewards those who earnestly seek him. (Hebrews 11:1,6)

This also accounts for the fact that unbelievers can't see him. They haven't experienced the reality of God for themselves. They're still dead to him, because the Spirit hasn't made them alive in their souls. They might know *about* God from others – even from the testimony of others – but they themselves have never met God personally.

This spiritual skill of faith enables us to see the truth about Jesus. Even though on the outside he may not look all that impressive (which is by his own choice, by the way) through faith we can see who he really is and what he's really doing. Faith takes away the veil from our eyes so that we can see the glory of God in Christ. The Bible says that God put his fullness in Jesus, and through faith we can see God in him.

Now there are two steps to the Father's testimony about the Son that will bring us face to face with the reality of God's power in him:

- **First,** God displayed his power in Jesus. We've already seen how the Father did miraculous things through Jesus in his ministry. But if anybody needed more confirmation of the Father's backing and intentions, they got it in the resurrection of Christ:

  > ... the gospel he promised beforehand through his Prophets in the Holy Scriptures regarding his Son, who as to his human nature

was a descendant of David, and who through the Spirit of holiness was declared with power to be the Son of God by his resurrection from the dead: Jesus Christ our Lord. (Romans 1:2-4)

The resurrection of Christ accomplished several things that were crucial for the life of the Church. *One*, he destroyed the power of sin and death over God's people. Because Jesus died, we don't have to now. Sin has no more authority over us.

Two, since God raised Jesus back to life – to an indestructible, eternal life – we too will have that. God made his people one with Christ, so that everything that happened to him will happen to us too. Now that he will never die again, we can look forward to eternal life in him.

What happened after the resurrection is even more important. If Jesus had only come back from the dead, that would have accomplished the deed in himself but it wouldn't have spread out to the rest of God's people. He had to *ascend to Heaven* for the next step to occur. It's from his position at the right hand of God, on the throne of the universe, that he sends his Spirit of life and light to the entire Church, all over the world and throughout history. From there the power of what he had done gets distributed to the rest of us.

Both these events were due to the hand of the Father. The Father raised him from the dead, and the Father raised him on high to the throne of grace. As Jesus prophesied about all these things in his ministry, those who heard him – disciples and Pharisees alike – no doubt wondered if it were really true. But when God did it so powerfully, at least the disciples didn't doubt anymore! They got a graphic confirmation from the Father that everything Jesus promised did and will come true. If they didn't believe Jesus before, they did after the Spirit came on them in power – from the hand of Christ himself from his throne in Heaven.

- **Second,** the Father applies all these spiritual realities in our hearts now. It would have made an interesting story in itself (and many people still only look at it as a fascinating myth) but God wasn't interested in entertaining us. Jesus returned to Heaven to save us. He fully intends to apply the powers of Heaven, which he ascended to take hold of, to our souls. Now *we* are going to change as a result.

And this too is the Father's testimony to us that Jesus really is what the Bible claims he is. Jesus is there in Heaven now, interceding on our behalf, getting spiritual blessings from the Father for his people. For those who don't believe that the Father will honor Jesus' requests, imagine their surprise when they take his challenge seriously!

> In that day you will no longer ask me anything. I tell you the truth, my Father will give you whatever you ask in my name. (John 16:23)

When God actually answers a specific prayer of yours, after taking Jesus at his word and coming to the Father with your request, isn't that a powerful testimony that Jesus knows what he's talking about? That he really did fix the breach between God and us, and restored our relationship with the Father? The Father honors his Son by fulfilling Jesus' promises to us. That again is the Father's testimony behind the truth of Jesus' words and works.

> The Spirit himself testifies with our spirit that we are God's children. (Romans 8:16)

Answers to the mysteries

The Apostles talked about the "mystery" of the Gospel. What they were referring to was this fact that what we *hear* about Jesus doesn't match with what we *see* in him. The humble carpenter doesn't appear to be the Savior of the world! The Jews were amazed and offended with his claims, because he didn't appear to be what he claimed to be.

It was the Father's business, therefore, to make the mystery of Christ plain not only to his own people the Jews but also to the rest of the world:

> The promise is for you and your children and for all who are far off – for all whom the Lord our God will call. (Acts 2:39)

And that's why God showed the solution to the mystery of Christ to the Apostles. Paul claims that he now has insight into God's mysteries, and he can now declare the true message of the Gospel of Christ to the world. And he claimed of himself that God called him to this ministry, to reveal the mystery of Christ to the Church:

> Surely you have heard about the administration of God's grace that was given to me for you, that is, the mystery made known to me by revelation, as I have already written briefly. In reading this, then, you will be able to understand my insight into the mystery of Christ, which was not made known to men in other generations as it has now been revealed by the Spirit to God's holy Apostles and Prophets. This mystery is that through the gospel the Gentiles are heirs together with Israel, members together of one body, and sharers together in the promise in Christ Jesus. I became a servant of this gospel by the gift of God's grace given me through the working of his power. Although I am less than the least of all God's people, this grace was given me: to preach to the Gentiles the unsearchable riches of Christ, and to make plain to

everyone the administration of this mystery, which for ages past was kept hidden in God, who created all things. His intent was that now, through the church, the manifold wisdom of God should be made known to the rulers and authorities in the heavenly realms, according to his eternal purpose which he accomplished in Christ Jesus our Lord. In him and through faith in him we may approach God with freedom and confidence. (Ephesians 3:2-12)

I have become its servant by the commission God gave me to present to you the word of God in its fullness – the mystery that has been kept hidden for ages and generations, but is now disclosed to the saints. To them God has chosen to make known among the Gentiles the glorious riches of this mystery, which is Christ in you, the hope of glory. (Colossians 1:25-27)

The Witness of the Apostles

The coming of Christ was an event that demanded to be witnessed; it could not have happened in obscurity without someone being there to see it. When royalty goes somewhere – since they are not commoners – everything they do has great significance for the kingdom, even if they just want to get away for a vacation! When Jesus came, it wasn't just a visit – it was the greatest and potentially the most explosive event in the history of the universe!

The problem, however, is that he came almost incognito. Almost nobody knew who he really was. He set aside his glory that he had with the Father in Heaven, and "being made in human likeness" (Philippians 2:7) became one of us: the son of a poor carpenter in an obscure village in Palestine. He did this for a reason, of course: he didn't want to make a physical show of who he was; he wanted us to grasp his greatness by faith, not by sight.

The Apostles were witnesses of the life and ministry of Christ. They lived with him, worked with him, listened to him, and watched him as he taught and worked miracles through the countryside. At the time they probably didn't realize the important role they would play in the Church; but actually they were witnesses of the true nature of the Messiah. While everyone else was wondering who Jesus was, the disciples were given a clear vision. For them the mystery was swept aside and they saw his glory.

The definition of the word *apostle* is "the one sent out." But if we use just this definition, then many teachers in the Church today might feel that they are also apostles – which some do. But the Scripture adds another dimension to the definition. Since Judas had

The witness of the Apostles – 187

betrayed the Lord and killed himself, the rest of the disciples decided to choose another man to take his place. They laid down a certain qualification, however, for an apostle – whoever was chosen *had* to be a witness of Christ's life and ministry.

> Therefore it is necessary to choose one of the men who have been with us the whole time the Lord Jesus went in and out among us, beginning from John's baptism to the time when Jesus was taken up from us. For one of these must become a witness with us of his resurrection. (Acts 1:21-22)

There's a lot of depth to this verse. Essentially the Apostles were to testify of Christ's resurrection, which is the central event of the Gospel. But not just anybody who saw the resurrection could be an apostle. It must be someone who also witnessed the entire ministry of Christ. Therefore, only a man who knew the events of the life of Christ would understand the point of the resurrection, and the resurrection would also shed light on the events of Christ's life that he witnessed.

John also describes the unique position of an apostle:

> That which was from the beginning, which we have heard, which we have seen with our eyes, which we have looked at and our hands have touched – this we proclaim concerning the Word of life. The life appeared; we have seen it and testify to it, and we proclaim to you the eternal life, which was with the Father and has appeared to us. We proclaim to you what we have seen and heard, so that you also may have fellowship with us. And our fellowship is with the Father and with his Son, Jesus Christ. (1 John 1:1-3)

The reason they had to be qualified witnesses is, as we have seen, that the life of Christ was so startling, it was so unexpected and mysterious, that there had to be someone who saw it to assure us that it really was the Son of God come in the flesh. We can doubt someone's ideas and opinions, but we can't doubt an eyewitness without calling him a liar. His testimony becomes invaluable if we want to know what really happened.

The disciples spent over three years with Christ. They watched him and listened to him as he did the works of God. They slowly came to understand who he really was; it didn't come to them overnight. This in itself shows us that what they were witnessing was not of this world. Christ was a man, but he was also *the Son of God* – and that means that there are deep spiritual realities involved in his ministry, and we need the Spirit of God to reveal them to us. Understanding Jesus doesn't come easily, as if we only need to put in a little effort to understand the point about him. The Pharisees, for example, also saw things that Christ did, yet *they* didn't see the deeper level at work like the disciples did.

What did the disciples see in Christ?

- **The God of the Old Testament** – Jesus was careful to show the disciples the *same God* that they had learned about from their Scriptures. We often miss this fact, because we think that Jesus came to do a new thing – to show us something different about God that the Old Testament doesn't show us. This is why many people don't bother to study the Old Testament: they think that the New Testament sets aside the Old, as if we don't need the Old anymore.

The disciples themselves realized that they were witnessing the Old Testament God first-hand. Jesus did the same works as God, he taught the same truths, he called his people in the same ways. For example, he kept insisting that he did the *works* of God, and that should be proof of who he really was and who was behind his ministry:

> I have testimony weightier than that of John. For the very work that the Father has given me to finish, and which I am doing, testifies that the Father has sent me. (John 5:36)

> Don't you believe that I am in the Father, and that the Father is in me? The words I say to you are not just my own. Rather, it is the Father, living in me, who is doing his work. (John 14:10)

What were his works? Jesus taught the people of God about the kingdom, and about their responsibilities in the kingdom, just as God had done from the days of Moses, through the Kingdom of David, all through the ministry of the Prophets. Jesus fed his people, just as God had done in the wilderness. Jesus ruled over his people, laying out his laws for them to obey, just as God had done on Mt. Sinai and through the reign of King David. Jesus protected his people from their enemies, just as God did from the Philistines and others. Jesus led his people into the new Promised Land, just as God did the Israelites.

One important point to realize is that Jesus did these things in the *same way* that God did them in the Old Testament. This is the way we can know that we are dealing with the same God. Other gods won't do these things in this way, because they *can't*. The Apostles were careful to point out this fact to us – so, these are what most impressed them during their time spent with him:

The spoken Word: Before doing any work of creation, blessing or punishment, God always issues his Word of command, promise or rebuke. The Word comes first, then the work. There are several reasons for this: **first**, he shows us that he knows what he's going to do, ahead of time, even though it's impossible. What better way to display his divine wisdom and power! "I make known the end from the beginning, from ancient times, what is still to come. I say: My purpose will stand, and I will do all that I please." (Isaiah 46:10)

Second, he wants us to live by faith, not by sight. He wants us to trust in what *he says*, not in what *we see*. If we live only by what we see, our lives will be empty – because sin and death will fill our world and they can't do us any good. For example, Jesus remarked that the Jews followed him for the wrong reasons instead of the right ones – they liked him only because he gave them physical bread to eat, instead of trusting in him for spiritual bread.

> I tell you the truth, you are looking for me, not because you saw miraculous signs but because you ate the loaves and had your fill. Do not work for food that spoils, but for food that endures to eternal life, which the Son of Man will give you. On him God the Father has placed his seal of approval. (John 6:26-27)

He did his work through the power of the Spirit: When God does anything in this world, he works through the Holy Spirit; he has always done so. This may seem strange, because not many people are aware of how important the Spirit is in the scheme of things. But because of the requirements of the work, and the nature of the work, the Spirit is the most appropriate agent for all of God's works.

For example, the Spirit was there at the beginning of the world: "The Spirit of God was hovering over the waters." (Genesis 1:2) This should tell us something about the nature of the physical world: that it was created at the hands of a spiritual God, according to spiritual principles, for spiritual purposes. We are closing our eyes to the real nature of our world if we only look at material things and ignore the spiritual foundation of the world, laid down by the Spirit of God at the beginning.

The Prophets, as we have seen, all spoke and knew what to say by the Spirit of God. Zechariah tells us God's strategy: God works through the Spirit – "Not by might nor by power, but by my Spirit, says the LORD Almighty." (Zechariah 4:6)

If this is such an important principle in all of God's works, we would expect to see the same in Christ's ministry – that is, if he really is the Son of God. And in fact we do. The Apostles were careful to record for us the work of the Spirit in everything that Jesus did. At the very beginning of his life we learn that the Spirit brought about his miraculous birth; the angel told his mother that –

> The Holy Spirit will come upon you, and the power of the Most High will overshadow you. So the holy one to be born will be called the Son of God. (Luke 1:35)

When Jesus was baptized by John, the Spirit came down on him in power, beginning a ministry that would be full of miracles and the power of God. He was tempted by the devil but was "full of the Holy Spirit" (Luke 4:1) and so able to deal with the problem. He cast out devils by the Spirit of God. He opened the minds of his disciples by the revealing power of the Spirit. He healed people from all kinds of diseases, and even raised some from the dead. All that he did and said came through the power and revelation of the Spirit:

> The Spirit of the Lord is on me, because he has anointed me to preach good news to the poor. He has sent me to proclaim freedom for the prisoners and recovery of sight for the blind, to release the oppressed, to proclaim the year of the Lord's favor. (Luke 4:18-19)

Many people since his day have doubted that Jesus really did all these amazing things. Skeptics are sure that nobody can work miracles like these, or really know the mind of God. But the Apostles testify to the fact that Jesus did, in fact, work these miracles and teach the truth about God – because he was filled with the Spirit who gave him the power and wisdom to do it. We may not know how he did such things, but the Apostles knew.

He got glory from what he did: God always works for his glory. Glory is simply this: *who gets the credit*? You can turn to any of the works of the Lord in the Old Testament and you will find God drawing our attention to himself: *he* works miracles, *he* loves his people, *he* destroys his enemies, *he* is wisdom, *he* is holy. Men and women are always put in their proper place in relation to this amazing God: they are humble, repentant, hard-hearted, undeserving, ignorant, weak and helpless, tyrannical, wicked, faithful, trusting in God, and so on. But none of them could save themselves, none of them had the answers to their problems, none of them got away with any wickedness. God alone gets the glory for any good that we have in life. And he will certainly give the wicked what they deserve.

Jesus was the same way. He demanded glory; he would have nobody misunderstanding who he really was. For example, what kind of claim is he making about himself in this statement?

> If you do not believe that I am the one I claim to be, you will indeed die in your sins. (John 8:24)

He claims to be the Savior; he claims that there is no other salvation from sin than himself. He claims to be able to rescue us from death itself. In fact, he claims to be something that terrifies the human heart, because sinners don't naturally want to admit that he's the Holy One of God. Now either Jesus was filled with unspeakable pride, or he's drawing our attention to him as the only way to life. This is the Glory of God at work.

The Apostles showed us his glory at every turn in the story. The way he was born, the way he taught and worked miracles, the way he dealt with the enemy, the way he died, the way he launched the new Church, the way he continues to support the Church and make it live and grow – we learn how vast and powerful and full of love the Son of God really is. We also learn that we can do none of these things without him, and that we desperately need him. In other words, the hero of the Apostles' story is always Jesus. One comes away from the New Testament convinced that we need him.

The result was something that he was pleased with: This is a subtle aspect to God's works that many people often miss. We know that God works in a different *way* than we do, but we don't often realize that he works for different *goals* as well. We are usually only satisfied with results that we can see and touch. God, however, works on a kingdom that can't be seen or touched with the physical senses. And he's disappointed when his people are content with physical treasures, and we have so little interest in his spiritual kingdom.

For example, I believe that we often miss the point of the words "God saw all that he had made, and it was *very good*" (Genesis 1:31) in the story of Creation. What does "very good" mean? Good for *us*? Beautiful to look at? Perfect in workmanship? It's true that the world was all these things, but God was after something much more important than our well-being. The world was made in such a way that it reflected his *glory* – and as it does that, he's happy with it. "The heavens declare the glory of God; the skies proclaim the work of his hands." (Psalm 19:1)

There are other instances of God aiming at spiritual goals and often mystifying people in the process. For example, it looked as if he was rejecting his own people when he sent them away in defeat to Babylon, and allowed the enemy to destroy Jerusalem, including the holy Temple. But he sacrificed the physical side of the covenant in order to gain a spiritual victory: he broke the back of idol worship among the Jews, a wickedness that they had wallowed in like pigs for generations. They came back from Exile a chastened people who never turned to false gods again. If they had to suffer in order to become holy, that end justified the means used, in God's eyes.

Jesus showed the same divine characteristic in his dealings with people. He was not primarily after their physical well-being (though he healed many of their illnesses). His miracles were designed to draw their *hearts* to him as the Son of God; he saved their bodies as a proof that he could also save their souls. He said as much to the Pharisees, who doubted his true mission:

> When Jesus saw their faith, he said to the paralytic, "Son, your sins are forgiven." Now some teachers of the law were sitting there, thinking to themselves, "Why does this fellow talk like that? He's blaspheming! Who can forgive sins but God alone?" Immediately Jesus knew in his spirit that this was what they were thinking in their hearts, and he said to them, "Why are you thinking these things? Which is easier: to say to the paralytic, 'Your

sins are forgiven,' or to say, 'Get up, take your mat and walk'? But that you may know that the Son of Man has authority on earth to forgive sins...." He said to the paralytic, "I tell you, get up, take your mat and go home." He got up, took his mat and walked out in full view of them all. This amazed everyone and they praised God, saying, "We have never seen anything like this!" (Mark 2:5-12)

There were many other occasions that revealed a divine mission that was often at odds with human opinions. Peter rebuked Jesus for willingly going to the cross – and Jesus accused him of not knowing God's way of doing things. The rich young man got counsel from Jesus to sell all his riches and *then* follow the Lord (not what we would have told him!). But Jesus knew that this course of action would save the man's soul. Jesus counseled all of us to lay up treasures in Heaven, not on earth; to give away our wealth so that we might be welcomed in Heaven; that we should deny ourselves and carry our cross if we want to live. And in the story of the tax collector and the Pharisee, with whom was Jesus pleased?

The Pharisee stood up and prayed about himself: 'God, I thank you that I am not like other men – robbers, evildoers, adulterers – or even like this tax collector. I fast twice a week and give a tenth of all I get.' But the tax collector stood at a distance. He would not even look up to heaven, but beat his breast and said, 'God, have mercy on me, a sinner.' I tell you that this man, rather than the other, went home justified before God. For everyone who exalts himself will be humbled, and he who humbles himself will be exalted. (Luke 18:11-14)

The point is this: the Apostles testified that Jesus has the same goals and the same purposes in mind as did the God of the Old Testament.

The disciples carefully noted what Jesus did and how he did it, and recorded these things for the benefit of the Church. They didn't miss the significant details, nor did they create a story to suit their own notions of who Jesus was (as many in our day accuse them of doing!). They were faithful witnesses of the event when Israel's God came to visit them in person. Who will accuse them of lying about what they testify of? Jesus really is the Son of God; what he said and did is proof of that.

- **Miracles** – The stories of the miracles in the Gospels are an absolutely essential part of the Apostles' witness about Christ. Jesus came to do miracles. The job of the Apostles was to witness them, and record what happened. Without the miracle stories, we wouldn't have a Gospel to preach.

A miracle is an impossible thing come true. Nobody but God can do miracles (though the devil can fool people with his tricks and sleights of hand). In fact, this is the definition of a miracle:

A miracle is what God does directly, apart from natural means.

For example, we all know how to get bread to eat: We start with last year's grain, plant it, water it, hoe the weeds out, harvest it, grind it up, add other ingredients, bake it, and we have bread. But when God makes bread, he bypasses all the intermediate steps that we rely on and creates it out of nothing. He sent manna out of the sky, for instance, when his people needed bread in the desert. (Exodus 16) How did he do that? *Nobody knows.* It was a physical impossibility; we couldn't do it if we tried. When there's a need that the natural world, and man himself, can't fill, God bypasses the natural means and works a miracle to fill that need.

Jesus' entire ministry was filled with miracles. They were all clearly impossible events. In fact, this is why people don't believe that Jesus did such things – they aren't possible; our world doesn't work like that. Only a naïve child would believe that such things happened. So unless someone was there and actually saw them happen, we just won't believe it.

There's the whole point. Someone *was* there and saw them happen. *We* weren't there, it's true, but the disciples were just as reliable witnesses as we would have been: they too were unbelieving, ignorant, refusing to believe their eyes, self-righteous, thick-headed, self-centered, and highly opinionated! So Jesus worked miracle after miracle, proving to them over and over the divine power behind his work. Gradually they began to understand the point of this man who could do the impossible whenever he wanted – whenever the need arose.

Jesus did amazing things. We read the Gospels in such a casual way, as if miracles were normal fare in those days. If he were here in our age, the newspapers would cover their front pages daily with the staggering works of Christ. Every person across our nation would be talking about this worker of wonders. That's exactly what happened in his day:

> And when the demon was driven out, the man who had been mute spoke. The crowd was amazed and said, "Nothing like this has ever been seen in Israel." (Matthew 9:33)

> Jesus returned to Galilee in the power of the Spirit, and news about him spread through the whole countryside. (Luke 4:14)

Why are the miracles such an important part of the Gospel of Christ? *Because only God does miracles.* No man, no matter how holy or powerful or wise he may be, can do these impossible things. Man is forced to work under the constraints of the real world. Modern man is very clever, and has found almost "miraculous" ways of controlling his environment, but he still has to work according to physical laws. So when we see Jesus doing what only God can do, this tells us something crucial about him: that he's the Son of God, who does the works of God and speaks the very words of God. In this respect he is *not* like us.

> Why then do you accuse me of blasphemy because I said, 'I am God's Son'? Do not believe me unless I do what my Father does. But if I do it, even though you do not believe me, believe the miracles, that you may know and understand that the Father is in me, and I in the Father. (John 10:36-38)

We need to know this, because we need to know where to go when we need help – to the only one who can work miracles for us. There is much that we can't do for ourselves: we can't extend our lives, we can't protect ourselves against the world, we can't save ourselves from our sin, we can't reach Heaven – we can't even *see* Heaven! "No one can see the Kingdom of God unless he is born again." (John 3:3) As Jesus said, unless we believe that he's the miracle worker, and go to him for what we desperately need – a miracle of salvation – we will surely die. Many refuse to go to him for this miracle. It was said of people in his own hometown, "he did not do many miracles there because of their lack of faith." (Matthew 13:58)

The Apostles, therefore, knowing how crucial it is to our faith to see the true nature of the person and work of Christ, made no mistake in presenting him to us in the Gospels. They showed us his glory in all its majesty: commanding the dead to life, touching and healing, healing from a distance, stilling the storm waves, walking on water, turning water to fine wine, knowing men's thoughts. And they testify to these things as *eyewitnesses*. They were there; they saw these things happen. They were sane, level-headed, practical men who saw Jesus do the impossible. Who will call their testimony into question? Will we? We weren't there! Does our modern scientific outlook deny the possibility of such miracles? That's the very point about a miracle, however – Jesus went *around* scientific laws, something that we can't do, to do his will. We are not dealing with an ordinary man here; the Apostles are showing us God at work.

But the lesson about the miracles is not that Jesus did them to impress us with his power. If this is God – and that's what the miracles prove – then the next step in our faith is obvious:

> We must pay more careful attention, therefore, to what we have heard, so that we do not drift away. For if the message spoken by angels was binding, and every violation and disobedience received its just punishment, how shall we escape if we ignore such a great salvation? This salvation, which was first announced by the Lord, was confirmed to us by those who heard him. God also testified to it by *signs, wonders and various miracles*, and gifts of the Holy Spirit distributed according to his will. (Hebrews 2:1-4)

In other words, if Jesus did these physical miracles, then he's the one who can and will work spiritual miracles in our souls. He can do the impossible – like make a sinner into a saint, a rebel into a child of God, and Heaven into the eternal home for man.

- **The fulfillment of the prophecies** – We already looked at how important the prophecies of the Old Testament are as a testimony to Christ and his true nature. It's still possible, however, for people to doubt that the Prophets had Jesus of Nazareth in mind. After all, how in the world could a prophet look into the future and utter a prophecy about a single man out of the billions of people in history? Isn't it possible to interpret those prophecies as describing many different men, even the entire nation of Israel? Even if you have never had such suspicions about the Prophets, there have been many others who have.

That's where the Apostles come in. In a master stroke of historical documentation, they brought out the hundreds of Old Testament prophecies and proved that they were fulfilled in the words and works of Christ. *This is the man that the Prophets spoke of;* here is the proof that he fulfilled those prophecies, one by one, to demonstrate his divine nature and ministry.

The Apostles were well-versed in the Prophets, and lost no opportunity to point out when Jesus fulfilled another prophecy. For example, here are just a few of Matthew's testimonies of Christ fulfilling the Prophets:

> *All this took place to fulfill what the Lord had said through the prophet.* (Matthew 1:22)
>
> *And so was fulfilled what the Lord had said through the prophet.* (Matthew 2:15)
>
> *... to fulfill what was said through the prophet Isaiah.* (Matthew 4:14)
>
> *But this has all taken place that the writings of the Prophets might be fulfilled.* (Matthew 26:56)

Sometimes we may wonder why the Apostle thinks that Christ's action was a fulfillment of a prophecy. It seems to us that the prophecy could be interpreted in several ways, and what happened to Jesus doesn't appear to be the real meaning of the prophecy. For example, Matthew claims that Jesus' parents moving to Egypt to escape the wrath of Herod fulfilled the following prophecy:

> *When Israel was a child, I loved him, and out of Egypt I called my son. (Hosea 11:1,* see also *Matthew 2:15)*

On the surface it appears that the prophet is talking about Israel in Moses' day – they were an infant nation, a new people that he called out of the slavery in Egypt and brought into the Promised Land. Surely Hosea had that story in mind! But Matthew tells us that it's also about Christ as an infant! No matter what Hosea might have understood in his day, God (who spoke through Hosea by the Spirit) looked *forward* in time to when his *own* Son would come out of hiding in Egypt. Now we have something interesting here: even the Exodus of the Israelites out of Egypt was a type, a shadow, that teaches us about the more important event of Christ coming out of Egypt. Matthew forces us to change the way we have previously understood Scripture, because the point of *all* prophecy is Christ.

- **The Kingdom of God** – The Kingdom of God is one of the most important themes of the New Testament. All that we have said about Jesus so far would be impressive in itself, but nobody would have any reason to believe that it necessarily involves us today. But the Apostles saw an amazing thing unfold before them in the ministry of Jesus. They saw a vast spiritual kingdom taking shape that reaches out into all of history, through all nations and cultures. They saw and testified about a kingdom that includes us all.

The Old Testament, of course, is about the Kingdom of God over the Jews. At the very beginning of Jewish history, God announced that he was their God – and he would rule over them, they must abide by his Laws, and he would make them into a kingdom in which there would be peace and justice and righteousness. The kingdom experienced various degrees of success: under Joshua and David, for example, things went pretty well; but under most of the kings of Israel and Judah, the Israelites basically ignored God and did things their own way.

The Prophets knew (through the Spirit) that things couldn't go on this way. God hates sin; he simply will not tolerate a world where people rebel against his Law. And it's not as if he's acting like a tyrant! It's to man's benefit to submit to God's Law, and depend on God to provide what he needs. Only when people rebel against the King do they end up with misery and death on their hands. So the Prophets spoke of a day when God would put new life into his kingdom – through the work of Christ. We have already looked at some of those prophecies.

The disciples knew, once they realized who Jesus really was, that he was here to work on that Kingdom. They remembered the prophecies. What they didn't realize at first was the true nature of Christ's kingdom! They thought he came to set up an earthly kingdom, with his throne in Jerusalem, ruling over the entire earth with them as his special counselors:

> So when they met together, they asked him, "Lord, are you at this time going to restore the kingdom to Israel?" (Acts 1:6)

It wasn't until after his resurrection and the outpouring of the Spirit that they understood what kind of kingdom he had come to set up. In fact, he had begun the building of the kingdom right under their noses! As they wrote their testimonies of him, they remembered important events that revealed him at his work of building up the kingdom. They remembered that he started out his ministry with these words:

> After John was put in prison, Jesus went into Galilee, proclaiming the good news of God. "The time has come," he said. "The kingdom of God is near. Repent and believe the good news!" (Mark 1:14-15)

They remembered that he described what his kingdom would be like:

> After this, Jesus traveled about from one town and village to another, proclaiming the good news of the kingdom of God. (Luke 8:1)

They remembered that he laid the Law down in his Kingdom:

> For I tell you that unless your righteousness surpasses that of the Pharisees and the teachers of the Law, you will certainly not enter the Kingdom of Heaven. (Matthew 5:20)

They remembered that he challenged the kingdoms of this world, that he proclaimed himself King of all other kings:

> You are right in saying that I am a king. In fact, for this reason I was born, and for this I came into the world, to testify to the truth. Everyone on the side of truth listens to me. (John 18:37)

They remembered the King traveling around and making things right in his Kingdom: calling people into it as new citizens, healing the hurts, defeating his enemies, feeding the hungry, lifting up the downtrodden:

> Jesus went through all the towns and villages, teaching in their synagogues, preaching the good news of the Kingdom and healing every disease and sickness. (Matthew 9:34)

They also remembered that he promised a vast spiritual treasury to his followers, part of a world that's not of this physical world:

> Do not store up for yourselves treasures on earth, where moth and rust destroy, and where thieves break in and steal. But store up for yourselves treasures in Heaven, where moth and rust do not destroy, and where thieves do not break in and steal. For where your treasure is, there your heart will be also. (Matthew 6:19-20)

The point is that the Apostles realized that Jesus was building a spiritual, eternal, perfect kingdom that was all that the Old Testament kingdom promised to be and never was. It was only the beginning, to be sure, but they alert us to the *fact* – it exists now, and we are either inside or outside of Jesus' kingdom.

This is the truth

The Apostles testified about what they saw and heard. Unfortunately, many modern scholars have real doubts about the writings of the Apostles. They (the scholars, that is!) feel that the life of Christ is actually much simpler and less miraculous than the Gospels portray it. They think that the Apostles made the story more glamorous and added new ideas of divinity and miracles that aren't really true of Jesus. But, fortunately, we have an answer to that charge: essentially they are calling the Apostles liars. They had better be ready to back up their charge with facts!

At one point in their education, Jesus introduced the disciples to the way that they would witness about him to the world. In the story of Jesus feeding the 5000, they found themselves out in the middle of nowhere, with almost no food to eat and thousands of hungry people. The disciples asked Jesus to send everyone away to eat, and Jesus, out of compassion, wanted to feed them himself. He immediately turned to his disciples and said, "They do not need to go away. *You* give them something to eat." (Matthew 14:16) What follows is instructive. Without changing his mind, he took what little bread there was, prayed over it, and broke it. "Then he gave them to the disciples, and *the disciples* gave them to the people." (Matthew 14:19) This was special training for their future ministry. The point is this: they are to take what Christ gives them and give that to the people. No changes, no holding anything back, no substitutes – everything that they get from Jesus, they give to others. If they do it *that way*, they will be faithful workers.

Now, the testimony of the Apostles, especially in the Gospels, is either *lies* or a *faithful account of what they got from Jesus himself.* They were not trained to change or add anything to what they received. He wouldn't own them as his servants if they interfered in any way with him feeding his sheep. As it says in Proverbs, "A wicked messenger falls into trouble, but a trustworthy envoy brings healing." (Proverbs 13:17) Only if the Apostles gave us bread from Jesus' hand – in other words, were trustworthy and did what they were told to do ("You shall be my witnesses" – Acts 1:8) would they do us good.

Founded on the Spirit

The book of Acts is the record of the beginning and the growth of the Church, but it's careful to give credit where credit is due. The disciples watched Jesus go back to Heaven, and then they basically sat and waited until the next step in the process. That next step was crucial for their own testimony; they couldn't have done it otherwise. Even though they had seen Jesus, and they knew the important facts about him, and they could testify that they was the Son of God – the task they had before them required much more than that.

When the day of Pentecost came, they were all together in one place. Suddenly a sound like the blowing of a violent wind came from heaven and filled the whole house where they were sitting. They saw what seemed to be tongues of fire that separated and came to rest on each of them. All of them were filled with the Holy Spirit and began to speak in other tongues as the Spirit enabled them. (Acts 2:1-4)

The Holy Spirit is the key to the power of the Apostles' testimony of Christ. The Spirit does two things in God's kingdom: *first*, he enlightens us, or reveals the things of God so that we *can* see them; he opens the eyes of our soul so that we can see into Heaven. It's because of the Spirit that anybody can know God, whether Prophet or Apostle or modern Christian. *Second*, the Spirit empowers us. He takes ordinary people and turns them into powerful servants of the Most High. He turns their words into arrows of conviction that pierce the hearts of sinners. Mortals are transformed into skillful and unerring builders of the eternal kingdom of God. When they work, miracles happen; the only way we can account for what happens is that the Spirit of God is working mightily through them.

This happened at Pentecost. Peter preached his first sermon and got astounding results – 3000 people learned the fear of the Lord and believed the Gospel. It's been said that Peter's sermon was nothing out of the ordinary for a preacher; the difference was that he was filled with the Spirit and *spoke the Word of God.*

God uses their testimony

Why are the Apostles so important as witnesses? Because they are literally the foundation of the entire Church. We depend on their testimony for every aspect of our spiritual life. Theirs wasn't just an interesting story from the past; without their witness, we would have no Christianity today. In fact, we can test how faithfully we ourselves are following Christ by how closely we stick to the witness of the Apostles. *They* laid down the guidelines, the fundamentals of our faith, the vision of Heaven, the love of God as they saw it in Christ.

> Consequently, you are no longer foreigners and aliens, but fellow citizens with God's people and members of God's household, built on the foundation of the Apostles and Prophets, with Christ Jesus himself as the chief cornerstone. (Ephesians 2:19-20)

The Scriptures that are our "rule of faith and practice" came from their hands. This means, then, that our entire religion is based on eyewitness accounts of a divine reality; there is nothing in it that is man-made, or of human reason.

Now do you understand why it's extremely important to stick to the testimony of the Apostles? *We must believe in the real God*; the Apostles tell us about the God that they saw. *We must do what God says to do*; the Apostles pass on to us what God commanded us. *We have to know what God plans to do to and for humanity*; the Apostles reveal those plans to us, having heard them from God's own lips. And if the Apostles didn't talk about it, it isn't very important to us spiritually. They laid the foundation that the Church *needs*.

> By the grace God has given me, I laid a foundation as an expert builder, and someone else is building on it. (1 Corinthians 3:10)

If we add anything to it, it only confuses the issue and puts us in grave danger of turning away from the only faith that can save us.

> But even if we or an angel from heaven should preach a gospel other than the one we preached to you, let him be eternally condemned! As we have already said, so now I say again: If anybody is preaching to you a gospel other than what you accepted, let him be eternally condemned! (Galatians 1:8-9)

> I warn everyone who hears the words of the prophecy of this book: If anyone adds anything to them, God will add to him the plagues described in this book. And if anyone takes words away from this book of prophecy, God will take away from him his share in

the tree of life and in the holy city, which are described in this book. (Revelation 22:18-19)

The witness of the Apostles makes the following things possible:

- **The Word of God.** The Apostles knew that their testimony was critical to the salvation of the people of God. It may appear to us that they were pretty arrogant, claiming as they did that their words were God's own words. But what were they to do? Their testimony gives life to the dead; they did indeed have the very words of God, full of power to heal and save and make new. That's why they found the boldness to stand up and proclaim the Gospel, even if others did take offense at their boldness. They cannot deny us what God gave them to pass on to us.

Paul appreciated the Thessalonians for their faith in his ministry:

> And we also thank God continually because, when you received the word of God, which you heard from us, you accepted it not as the word of men, *but as it actually is, the word of God,* which is at work in you who believe. (1 Thessalonians 2:13)

In other words, they knew that it wasn't Paul speaking to them, but their God. They obeyed what they heard, even though it did come through the lips of a fellow sinner.

The testimony of the Apostles quickly rose to the status of holy Scripture – not by a misguided adoration of ignorant followers, but by the claims of the Apostles themselves. Peter says this about Paul's writings:

> Bear in mind that our Lord's patience means salvation, just as our dear brother Paul

also wrote you with the wisdom that God gave him. He writes the same way in all his letters, speaking in them of these matters. His letters contain some things that are hard to understand, which ignorant and unstable people distort, *as they do the other Scriptures*, to their own destruction. (2 Peter 3:15-16)

This means that our New Testament is *a collection of testimonies written by men who saw and heard God*. Someone may deny the truth of the New Testament, but only by calling the Apostles liars.

- **Conversions.** When we read the stories of great men in history, we may get excited or motivated ourselves, and we may apply the lessons of their lives to our own circumstances. But when we read the testimony of the Apostles about Christ, we get converted. Obviously this isn't an ordinary history, or even an ordinary book: there is power in this message, the same kind of power that spoke at the beginning of time and created the universe out of nothing.

You can't argue with results. Modern skeptics frown on taking the stories of Jesus seriously, especially the miracles. They think it's foolish to trust in someone who lived 2000 years ago. Yet people are still reading the Gospels and finding new life there. They are faced with a living God, someone who still speaks to the heart of man and demands obedience. They hear the commands of God and their consciences hurt with the memory of how they have offended that God. They see hope in Jesus, and reach out to him and find forgiveness from him. They suddenly see a new spiritual world that they didn't know existed, and they start living according to new realities that other people aren't aware of. In short, a person changes from the inside out – by reading the testimony of the Apostles.

Most people know that something like that will happen if they read the New Testament; that's why they refuse to read it. They don't want to change! They are afraid of a book that has so much power over the human heart. They don't want to put themselves within range of its power. Their fear of the Bible is an impressive proof of its truth.

> This is the verdict: Light has come into the world, but men loved darkness instead of light because their deeds were evil. Everyone who does evil hates the light, and will not come into the light for fear that his deeds will be exposed. But whoever lives by the truth comes into the light, so that it may be seen plainly that what he has done has been done through God. (John 3:19-21)

The Apostles, through the revelation of the Spirit, not only knew that their message would transform lives, they knew the results of the transformation. They described the holy God and, since God will have a holy people, our own process of sanctification. We don't have to guess what God wants us to be, because he will work the message of the New Testament into our hearts to conform us to his image. We will, by the command and power of God, become saints – true followers of Christ as the Apostles describe it.

- **The giving of the Spirit.** We learn from the book of Acts that a peculiar thing happened wherever the Apostles ministered to people. Let's take Cornelius as an example. When Peter went in obedience to God to Cornelius' house, he had grave misgivings about the results. Weren't these Gentiles? Wasn't it accepted in Jewish circles that the Gentiles would never share in the inheritance of the Jews? But he preached to them anyway, and this is his account of what happened:

As I began to speak, the Holy Spirit came on them as he had come on us at the beginning. Then I remembered what the Lord had said: 'John baptized with water, but you will be baptized with the Holy Spirit.' So if God gave them the same gift as he gave us, who believed in the Lord Jesus Christ, who was I to think that I could oppose God? (Acts 11:15-17)

This wasn't the first time that such a thing happened: on Pentecost the Spirit came upon thousands of Jews who listened to Peter's preaching. But through Cornelius the Apostles learned that God uses the same method for both Jews and Gentiles – through the Apostles preaching the Word of God, the Spirit will come in power and convert their hearers. It's been the same ever since. The Church grows (an activity of the Spirit) based on the Word of the Apostles, like seed growing in fertile soil.

The Holy Spirit is called "the Spirit of Truth" (John 14:17) because he constantly attends the preaching and teaching of the Word. It's because of the Spirit that we understand the message of the Bible; in fact, it's because of the Spirit that the Bible is even preached! He makes the spiritual gifts possible in the Church, those Heavenly powers given to men that open up the glory of God to the Church. In the hands of the Spirit of God, the Bible becomes a powerful force that shapes our lives and changes the world:

> ... the sword of the Spirit, which is the word of God. (Ephesians 6:17)

> For the word of God is living and active. Sharper than any double-edged sword, it penetrates even to dividing soul and spirit, joints and marrow; it judges the thoughts and attitudes of the heart. Nothing in all creation is hidden from God's sight. Everything is

uncovered and laid bare before the eyes of him to whom we must give account. (Hebrews 4:12-13)

One more essential point about the Bible. The Apostles wrote things that are simply impossible to believe – a God who took on flesh, who died for our sins, who does miracles, who prepares a place in Heaven for us. And they told us, by the authority of God, about Heaven's impossible standards: we must be perfect, even as God is perfect. How in the world are people going to believe these things, let alone live by them? How can God expect us to live the impossible message of the New Testament? Again, this is where the Spirit comes in. As we read, the Spirit empowers us to live this life-giving story. He transforms us into the image of Christ, which is the message of the apostolic witness. The Spirit gives us the wisdom and the ability to live in righteousness, "in order that the righteous requirements of the Law might be fully met in us, who do not live according to the sinful nature but according to the Spirit." (Romans 8:4)

Did the Apostles realize that their words would be used of God in people's lives to literally create a new nation, an eternal Church down through the ages? Obviously – the references we have been looking at are their own testimony to the fact! They testified to what they knew: the power of the Word of God, and the intention of the Spirit to use *their words* to build the Church of Christ.

- **Faith.** What happens when we read the testimony of the Apostles? One of two things: we either reject the message we hear, or we respond in faith. The message is strange, and impossible to believe, as far as human reason can make of it. That's why most people reject their testimony, though they have no good reason for doing so. What they end up doing, therefore, is calling the Apostles liars – though they wouldn't plainly say that! But some hear the message and feel a strange eagerness in their hearts to accept the truth of it. The truth enlightens their minds and hearts, like a light shining out of Heaven, making plain what used to be dark and confusing. Belief in the message comes naturally, easily – they can't deny what they hear any more than they can deny their own existence.

Faith is not what most people think it is. It isn't believing in some truth, that a doctrine is correct. Faith is not hoping that what you want will come true. True faith isn't a natural action of a sinful human's heart. We long ago lost the ability to trust God in spiritual matters. So the work of the Spirit in our day is to give us the ability to reach out and grasp the reality of God's world, to see it as it really is, and live as though it's a real foundation under our feet and the goal of our lives.

> For it is by grace you have been saved, through faith – and this not from yourselves, it is the gift of God – not by works, so that no one can boast. For we are God's workmanship, created in Christ Jesus to do good works, which God prepared in advance for us to do. (Ephesians 2:8-10)

Now the ultimate purpose in the message of the Apostles is that we might hear and believe the truth about Christ.

> But these are written that you may believe that Jesus is the Christ, the Son of God, and that by believing you may have life in his name. (John 20:31)

Does this in fact happen? Is this the way that God designed for us to have faith? Does faith come by hearing the Word?

Consequently, faith comes from hearing the message, and the message is heard through the word of Christ. (Romans 10:17)

This accounts for the otherwise mysterious faithfulness in Christians to the New Testament that so frustrates unbelievers. Christians have no earthly reason to believe the Apostles' testimonies about Christ; yet they will willingly die for them.

For you did not receive a spirit that makes you a slave again to fear, but you received the Spirit of sonship. And by him we cry, "Abba, Father." The Spirit himself testifies with our spirit that we are God's children. (Romans 8:15-16)

Hostile Witnesses

Strangely enough, the case for the reality of God and his works has an unexpected benefactor – the *hostile witness*. This is the person who doesn't want to help God at all in anything that he does, yet he can't help himself – he has to admit that what God says is true. Being an unwilling witness, he can't deny that God is real without lying. And his testimony is often far more powerful than those who are on God's side already, because people are doubly impressed with someone who doesn't *want* to admit that God is right, but he *has* to admit it because his experience proves otherwise.

What we want to do is analyze the clever legal move that God made in bringing in hostile witnesses to his courtroom, and examine the testimony of some of the better known examples in Scripture.

What is a hostile witness?

In a courtroom case, the job of proving the defendant guilty or innocent requires a lot of time, careful planning, and resources. The prosecuting attorney and the defense attorney has to use whatever they can find to prove their cases. As we've already seen, eyewitness testimony is far more valuable to a case than physical evidence, because evidence can be made to support just about any theory; but eyewitnesses can tell us exactly what they saw happen.

Sometimes the attorney can use an unexpected source of facts to support his case: the hostile witness. Let's use an example to illustrate the point. Let's say that a man was accused of murder. The defense of course will bring in his parents as character witnesses, who will testify about how their son is a fine example of morality and filial love. But the prosecuting attorney can also call the parents as witnesses to support *his* case. He can *make* them testify about whether their son was at home at the time of the crime. Of course the man's parents don't want to say anything that will put him in jeopardy; and they certainly won't give out that information willingly – often the prosecutor has to pry it out of them. But under penalty of law, the parents have to answer the attorney's questions about their son's whereabouts. They are friendly with the defendant, but they are *hostile* to what the prosecuting attorney is trying to do. However, it could end up that their testimony helps to seal their own son's doom, much to their chagrin.

As the law sees it, the testimony of a hostile witness is particularly powerful. The witness *wants* to testify otherwise; he has reasons to be reluctant to give the opposition any support at all. But since he's compelled to tell the truth, what he has to say about the matter impresses the court – he's supporting the very thing he hates to support. Someone who is hostile to the opposition would be more willing to lie about what he knows, instead of telling the truth that would hurt his own cause. So when he gives testimony that damages his own case, we can be pretty well assured that what he said happened, really did happen.

We can expect the Lord to use the same kind of testimony in his case about who he is. Naturally speaking, we are all reluctant to admit anything true about God, since that would mean we are in deep trouble about our sins. If this God is real, then we are rebels (as the Bible testifies) and God has already committed himself to dealing severely with our rebellion. So we are going to be unwilling to help his cause against us in any way; we love our lives too much to risk them in his court of inquiry. Therefore the Lord will bring witnesses against us, and he is going to use hostile witnesses – mainly because so few people are willing ones!

What he wants to convince us of, remember, is that he is real. He does real things on earth. He's the Creator who made the world in the first place. He's the Judge, the Redeemer, the miracle-worker, the Holy One, the King of kings, the Lord of the Heavenly hosts. He answers prayer. He punishes the wicked for their sins. And naturally if all these things are true about him, that means we need to change our way of living accordingly. So in order to convince us that he is real and all these things about him are true, he brings in eyewitnesses to prove his case.

The hostile witnesses that he has picked are particularly effective ones. God chose some of the hardest, most wicked, most ignorant of men and women to witness his works. They had absolutely no interest in the true God; they often worshipped false gods and did everything possible to avoid the real God. Even when they witnessed the true God at work, and gave their unwilling testimony in his favor, they went back to their false gods and wickedness as soon as possible. In other words, just because God used their testimony to support his cause, that didn't make them believers in him – which is a particularly sobering thought for the rest of us.

What do they testify about?

There are particular things about God that hostile witnesses will be good for. They of course aren't interested in his love, or his mercy, or his forgiveness of sin. They don't know by experience the best things about God that his children are most interested in. But there are many other aspects about God that they can testify about (unwillingly, of course!) that will not only strengthen the faith of the people of God, but ought to give unbelievers something to think about.

Also, these witnesses – because their testimony is so impressive and convincing – deal with issues that people most often dishonor God's Name over. For example, there have been many people in history that doubt that God is actually just and fair, considering all the human misery that exists the world over. They blame God whenever things go wrong, as if he could have prevented them from happening if he wanted to – so why didn't he want to? With those kinds of doubts about God's character, we need some sort of solid confirmation that God isn't irresponsible, or unjust, or lacks control. These hostile witnesses have something to say about that which should convince the most skeptical critic. After hearing their testimony, we should have a different opinion about the difficult issues of Heaven.

- **God's justice:** The way that people usually look at the issues of right and wrong is that they go by their own feelings and opinions. And, not surprisingly, everyone thinks that they will come out pretty well on Judgment Day. Nobody feels that they deserve Hell, and everyone at least has a glimmer of a hope (again, based on their own judgment) that if there is a Heaven and reward for the righteous, they should get at least part of it.

When you tell people that God has terrifyingly strict standards of morality, which will eliminate most people on earth from the Heavenly rewards, they react with horror, anger, and denial. God would never be so brutal to his own creatures, they say. Just look at all the love he showered on people who didn't deserve it!

But we don't have to wonder about whether God intends to strike down the wicked in wrath and destruction. We have eyewitnesses who can testify to that fact. They saw him rain down fire from Heaven, open up the earth beneath their feet, send hordes of the enemy in to destroy their cities and homes, inflict plagues on nations, drown their armies in the sea, and other terrifying miraculous disasters. The people who suffered these disasters don't have any problem at all believing this about God! They know first-hand that God will most certainly draw the line and punish the wicked when he chooses to do so.

We can argue about theory and doctrine all we want, and opinions are free and plentiful. But when it comes time to solve a question there's nothing like cold, hard facts – and the experience of those who lived through historical events. Though modern people don't want to believe in a God who won't hesitate to destroy the wicked, the people in Bible times found out the hard way that he most certainly will destroy them. For example, anybody from Jericho can testify to us that he saw the Israelites surround his city, blow on trumpets – and then, unaccountably, the walls collapsed! The entire city was put to death and destroyed. If we had that Jericho citizen here in court, he would be amazed at our unbelief. He would assure us that it all happened just as the Bible said it did, because he was there and experienced it. Not that he wanted it to happen, which would make his testimony particularly effective with us – he would rather it turned out differently!

The enemies of God can also testify to the fact that God gives justice to his people. For example, Solomon was once faced with the dilemma of what to do about a child that two women each claimed as her own. Due to God's wisdom that he gave Solomon, the dilemma was easily solved. The woman who was lying had to admit that Solomon's solution was amazingly perceptive of human nature, and that God did his will that day. She couldn't deny God's perfect justice. (1 Kings 3:16-28)

- **God's Holiness:** God is holy, which means that he can't abide sin, nor will he tolerate any of his creatures living in rebellion. "Holy" in the Old Testament Temple meant "set aside for God's use." Everything in the Temple was to be used only in the ceremonial service of the Temple, by the priests, for God's glory. Nothing that was sanctified, or made holy, was available for common use. So it is with all the parts of God's creation. He created everything to glorify him; he especially created man to glorify him by ruling over creation in his name, in his image, with his authority, working on his goals.

The Lord's holiness is so real that when we find ourselves in his presence, we feel like God is searching the inside of our hearts to see if we measure up to his standards. It's like a searchlight shining in the dark parts of our hearts and minds, in the areas that we thought were hidden to everyone but ourselves. God knows everything about us, because he has to know – he's the Creator and Judge, and he has to determine if we've done what he's commanded of us. The question with God is always this: do you measure up?

Sinners find this extremely unpleasant. Even the best of us quail at the thought of that searching test. Isaiah saw God in his holiness and was terrified:

> In the year that King Uzziah died, I saw the Lord seated on a throne, high and exalted, and the train of his robe filled the temple. Above him were seraphs, each with six wings: With two wings they covered their faces, with two they covered their feet, and with two they were flying. And they were calling to one another:
>
> "Holy, holy, holy is the LORD Almighty;
> the whole earth is full of his glory."
>
> At the sound of their voices the doorposts and thresholds shook and the temple was filled with smoke. "Woe to me!" I cried. "I am ruined! For I am a man of unclean lips, and I live among a people of unclean lips, and my eyes have seen the King, the LORD Almighty." (Isaiah 6:1-5)

He realized that his sin was a brilliant neon sign that flashed in God's eyes. We might be able to hide our sin from everyone else, but when we are in God's presence (really, not just in the empty ceremonies that we are too often content with) we stagger under the load of a guilty conscience.

Adam was the first to experience the sharp jab of guilt before the holy God. When God came to look for him and his wife, after they disobeyed him by eating the fruit of the Tree of the Knowledge of Good and Evil, they hid from him:

> Then the man and his wife heard the sound of the LORD God as he was walking in the garden in the cool of the day, and they hid from the

LORD God among the trees of the garden. (Genesis 3:8)

What they felt was this holiness of God; his holiness made them uncomfortable, and unwilling to be around him. And it's this that makes the wicked even in our day unwilling to even discuss the God of the Bible. They can't stand the purity of God, and the purity that he expects of them. They will talk about anything except the God of righteousness.

- **God's Power:** The most powerful things that we can imagine are as nothing to God. We can't imagine any power greater than, for example, the atomic bomb or the explosive power behind a supernova star. But God made all of these things, as powerful as they are; he was the source of their power. And if God is the creator of all things, how great is *his* power?

We have testimony about his power from his enemies. Again, they were forced to admit that God has overwhelming power to do anything he pleases. Nothing can stand in his way; nothing is able to resist him. For example, the Egyptians were witnesses of God's power. Even though they were the strongest nation on earth at the time, the Lord threw them around so easily that to him it was child's play to force the Egyptians into submission. Pharaoh knew that he was beaten by Israel's God, and had to admit it. He finally had to let them go to do what they wanted.

Unbelievers often ran into this power. They learned what kind of God they were up against when God unleashed that power against them. They knew that God tears nations down and lifts them up. They learned that God protects his people from their enemies. They saw this God perform amazing miracles against them – they found themselves on the wrong side of the stick. After they encountered this God, they never doubted what God could do. They went out of their way to avoid Israel's God! For example, Abimelech found out the hard way what kinds of things could happen to anybody who messes with one of the wives of the Israelites. (Genesis 20:1-18) The Philistines found out the hard way that they most definitely didn't want the ark of God in their communities. (1 Samuel 5:1-12)

Though Paul turned out to be one of Christ's Apostles, he started as the sworn enemy of the new Christian community. He "breathed threats" against them and did whatever he could to persecute the believers. So his own testimony of his encounter with a Jesus who proved not only to be real, but amazingly powerful, should make others think twice about lifting their hands against the Lord's anointed.

- **God's Authority:** Man loves to exercise authority. From the leaders of the country all the way down to the head of the house, authority is a big part of our lives. And just about anybody can claim to have authority of some kind. Even children try to "lord it over" their brothers and sisters. But what gives someone real authority is the power behind his claim. Can he *enforce* his authority? Can he make others obey him? That's what separates real authority from empty threats.

God has an authority that comes from who he is, not just what he claims. All his miracles are examples of his authority. We take authority upon ourselves; but God's authority is part of his nature. When he commands us, we discover that we can't help ourselves – we must obey him. Even if we don't actually do what he says, we will eventually be judged if we don't. And our guilty conscience is proof of the power of that obligation to God's authority. But usually when God commands something, he himself actually carries it out. God *will* do what he wants to do, and we *will* do what he tells us to do.

The story of Balaam is an excellent example of God's authority bulldozing through man's pitiful resistance and rebellion. Balaam was supposed to bring curses down on Israel as they passed through the land of Midian. But as he found out, the closer he got to the appointed time and place to do the job, the harder the way became. First God stopped his donkey with an angel, then God stopped Balaam himself. By the time he arrived in Midian to pronounce the curse, he was so terrified and spiritually bound that he was compelled to bless Israel, not curse them. (Numbers 22-24) Balaam had to admit that he was up against a power and authority stronger than his; he had no option but to obey God, though he himself didn't profess any belief in Israel's God. And to show that he definitely was no believer in God or friendly to God's intentions, he returned to his paganism after this happened.

Pharaoh too found himself confronting God. He thought he could manage his own country and make his own decisions – especially when it came to the slave laborers who belonged to the state. He found out differently. God's will overruled Pharaoh's will; God's authority has power, and Pharaoh's authority was only wishful thinking.

- **God's Goodness:** The enemies of God even have to admit that God is good to them. Though they hate to give him any credit for his goodness, they can't deny that they would be in bad shape if God weren't also looking after their well-being as well as his own people.

God gives freely to all, no matter what the state of their hearts are in and no matter what they've done against him. He gives food to all his creatures around the world, every day. (Psalm 145:8-9,15-16) He sends rain on the good and on the wicked. (Matthew 5:45) He gives us air to breathe, even if we use it to curse him. He lets the wicked live long lives, even if they never turn their thoughts to him or once repent of their sins against him. God is amazingly good to the undeserving. If he acted toward his enemies as we do, he would get rid of all the ungrateful wretches in the world who want nothing to do with him. Why shouldn't he? But the goodness of God runs deeper than that, fortunately, because there wouldn't be many of us left if he resorted to that!

The wicked can't deny that God heals the sick – Jesus healed ten lepers, even though only one came back to give God thanks. (Luke 17:11-19) The wicked can't deny that God feeds them daily – Jesus fed thousands of people during his ministry, the very people who cried for his blood later in Jerusalem. (Matthew 15:30-39) The wicked can't deny that God is patient with them, not wanting them to die but to come to a knowledge of the truth – Jesus taught the Jews for three years, putting up with their wickedness and ignorance and patiently explaining over and over the way of salvation. (2 Peter 3:9) On Judgment Day, everyone who stands before God's throne will have to admit that God gave them the blessings in life that they enjoyed, freely and willingly, whether they appreciated it or not.

Why are they hostile?

There are several reasons that so many people are hostile to God. You would think that after being so good to people, and doing terrifying things that should put fear in their hearts and cause them to repent of sin, that God wouldn't have any enemies left – just lots of people clamoring to get on his good side! But man's problem is deep-rooted in his nature, and it won't be changed easily. Most people would rather risk the unimaginable sufferings of Hell than lift a finger to plead with God for mercy.

> **Sin:** This is the biggest reason that people are hostile toward God. They love their sin, and they don't want anybody taking away their lusts and pleasures. And since God is holy, and hates sin, those who love their sin want to stay as far away from him as possible.
>
> John tells us that sinners hate the light that comes from God, because God reveals what they really are inside so that everyone can see:
>
>> This is the verdict: Light has come into the world, but men loved darkness instead of light

because their deeds were evil. Everyone who does evil hates the light, and will not come into the light for fear that his deeds will be exposed. (John 3:19-20)

For the same reason, unbelievers hate to read the Bible – because it too reveals what's in their hearts. They read about themselves there: it talks of sinners, people who rebel against God's authority, the commands God gave us that people aren't obeying, the good that God insists that we do which most people are ignorant about.

They also know that if they decide to take God seriously and do things his way for a change, they would *have* to give up their sins. There's something in the human heart that makes us all know that.

For this reason there are many who simply want nothing to do with God. Many people are religious, and they worship many kinds of gods; but they won't believe in or submit to the God of the Bible.

That's why it's particularly impressive to see God overruling their fear and hatred of him and *confronting their sins*, in spite of their best efforts to avoid him. Korah, for example, was determined to get some of the glory that Moses had as the leader of Israel. (Numbers 16) He talked himself into believing that he had the right to help lead the nation, that Moses was out of line claiming to be the sole prophet. If he could have, he would have talked everyone into believing that he had a rightful claim to leadership. But all of his clever arguments were proven empty when God slammed him with a brutal punishment: as far as God was concerned, Korah *sinned against God* with such thoughts. When God calls something sin, and then punishes the wicked for it, they have no room to deny it or blame God for being unfair to them. A punishment is an amazing argument against the wicked: they are *forced* to accept God's point of view of their actions.

God is the enemy: We have lots of problems in life, and we need a scapegoat to blame all these problems on. And since God claims to be in complete control of his world, who best to blame for the ills of life than the God who claims he has the power to do away with our problems!

We have all experienced the feeling of blaming God for the bad things that happen in life. Or at least we challenge him with the fact that he could have prevented them from happening; and if he's so powerful and loving, why didn't he prevent it? For example, many Jews still refuse to believe in God because the God they thought they believed in would never have let Nazi Germany exterminate 6 million Jews during World War II.

I know that people often go through amazing tragedies in their lives, and there doesn't seem to be any good reason that they had to endure such hardship. Many people are going through what Job went through: through no particular fault of his own, he lost his entire family and possessions, along with his health. He felt unfairly targeted by God for some reason that he knew nothing about. Why, God?

These unanswered questions make people hostile to God. They feel that he's the enemy, that he doesn't have their well-being at heart, that they don't want to know a God who would put them through this kind of suffering.

That's why God particularly wants to straighten out the record concerning these people. Jesus, for example, told his followers that people don't always suffer because of their own wickedness –

Now there were some present at that time who told Jesus about the Galileans whose blood Pilate had mixed with their sacrifices. Jesus answered, "Do you think that these Galileans were worse sinners than all the other Galileans because they suffered this way? I tell you, no! But unless you repent, you too will all perish. Or those eighteen who died when the tower in Siloam fell on them – do you think they were more guilty than all the others living in Jerusalem? I tell you, no! But unless you repent, you too will all perish." (Luke 13:1-5)

As he went along, he saw a man blind from birth. His disciples asked him, "Rabbi, who sinned, this man or his parents, that he was born blind?" "Neither this man nor his parents sinned," said Jesus, "but this happened so that the work of God might be displayed in his life." (John 9:1-3)

God has his own reasons for allowing people to go through suffering and hardship. Job eventually learned that in his own life. We can never blame God for what happens, because everything that God does or allows Satan to do is part of an overall perfect and righteous Kingdom. He knows exactly what he's doing; he isn't ignorant of the facts like we are. So when the Lord gets the opportunity to prove that we have no reason to blame him for our problems, he does it in such a way that "shuts the mouths" (Psalm 107:42) of those who want to dishonor him with slander.

We prefer false gods: When people love their sin, and have reasons to distrust or hate God for making them go through hardships, then they are more inclined to turn to false gods. False gods are handy things to have around. They don't control you, nor do they make any unreasonable demands on you, and they will let you believe whatever religious and moral doctrines that you want to believe. They are far less trouble than the real God, and much easier to get along with.

You understand, of course, that we're saying this tongue-in-cheek. There are no such things as false gods; all that is in people's heads. But whatever the reason, they would rather have any other god than the real God, who has ways that irritate them.

In the old days, people used to have stone, gold, silver, or wood gods on their shelves at home or in the community temple. They used to offer sacrifices to them to get answers to their problems. In our day, few people bow down to such gods, but actually we have the same situation. Modern man makes up what he wants his god to be and believes in that. Actually any god that is different from what the Bible says he is, is a false god – whether it's in someone's head or on his shelf.

Imagine their surprise when they meet the real God! They thought, and they desperately wished, that their own false god was real and that Israel's God was a fable. In our day we have many who wish that Israel's God was a myth and legend. But God delights in showing himself to them in powerful ways: answering prayer, converting hearts, frustrating the wicked, beating back the enemy. Pagans – those who believe in false gods – are constantly frustrated and speechless when they encounter the real God of the Bible.

Some hostile witnesses

Following are some of the hostile witnesses recorded in the Bible who found out for themselves that God is very real:

The Devil: The Devil is an interesting character. He is always the enemy of God; and though he has awesome powers that we little understand, God has constantly cornered, battled, limited, and defeated the Devil. God treats the Devil like a mad dog on a short leash: he lets Satan do awful things to people (like what he did to Job) but he limits the damage that Satan does. Satan can't do all that he wants because God is controlling his actions at all times.

Satan thought he was destroying the human race for good when he led Adam and Eve into sin; but God turned the situation around and prophesied a threat of doom on Satan himself:

> And I will put enmity between you and the woman, and between your offspring and hers; he will crush your head, and you will strike his heel. (Genesis 3:15)

And though that prophecy of doom has been millennia in the making, it is slowly and surely coming true. The Covenant with Abraham was the groundwork that God laid to "destroy the works of the Devil," and the rest of the Old Testament system of Temple and sacrifice was the blueprint to restore what Satan had hoped to destroy.

In the New Testament we read about Jesus' battle with Satan: it's a one-sided contest, because Jesus easily defeats Satan with weapons that only Heaven can provide. Even Jesus' disciples found out how easy it was to defeat the enemy:

> The seventy-two returned with joy and said, "Lord, even the demons submit to us in your name." (Luke 10:17)

And in the prophecy of the approaching final battle, we learn that Satan has no chance of survival when God comes to finally and completely destroy him and his forces:

> And the devil, who deceived them, was thrown into the lake of burning sulfur, where the beast and the false prophet had been thrown. They will be tormented day and night for ever and ever. (Revelation 20:10)

After this long history of battle with God, Satan can testify (of course unwillingly, but that's another aspect of God's victory over his enemies: he *will* get their unwilling testimony) that nobody wins against God. There is no power in Heaven or on earth that will prevail against God's holiness and power.

Pagans: In an interesting passage in Peter, we learn that those unbelievers whom we know *right now* will be forced to testify about the reality of God on Judgment Day – because of what they saw in *our* lives:

> Live such good lives among the pagans that, though they accuse you of doing wrong, they may see your good deeds and glorify God on the day he visits us. (1 Peter 2:12)

Whether we know it or not, the Spirit of God in the heart of the believer is at work changing the heart and life. A child of God is gradually looking more and more like Jesus. He doesn't love sin anymore, he turns away from fellowship with unbelievers and sinners and seeks the company of the righteous, he learns more about the truth of God, he crucifies the sin in his heart. The process may be gradual but it's real.

And while this is going on, people are watching. They knew us before we were converted, they've heard our testimony about meeting Jesus and changing allegiance, and they've been watching us. They of course don't want what we're into, but nevertheless their guilty conscience is keeping them alert to our progress. They want to see a failure, not a success! They want proof for their side of the argument: that this Christianity business isn't real, that it's all a myth, and that they aren't themselves obligated to take it seriously.

But when it does work, they don't know what to say. They have to admit that we have something that they don't have. While they're struggling with sin and its consequences, they see us freed from sin's burdens and walking in peace, joy and holiness. While they may have more of the world than Christians do, they don't have any of Heaven's spiritual treasures – and the difference is easy to see.

This is going to force them, on Judgment Day, to admit that we Christians were right all along and they were wrong. That will be a great day of justification for believers, and a day of embarrassment for those who refused to bend their knee to the God we worship and fear.

The Pharisees: Sometimes it's actually humorous how easily Jesus led the Pharisees around by their noses. Try as they might, they couldn't trap him or get him into trouble. They hated him, and they certainly had the legal and political clout to put him away. But at all times he showed that he controlled the situation, not they.

The reason that the Pharisees are hostile witnesses is that they themselves personally witnessed Jesus' miracles. They couldn't deny that he did what he did; they saw him do them.

> He looked around at them in anger and, deeply distressed at their stubborn hearts, said to the man, "Stretch out your hand." He stretched it out, and his hand was completely restored. Then the Pharisees went out and began to plot with the Herodians how they might kill Jesus. (Mark 3:5-6)

> Now the crowd that was with him when he called Lazarus from the tomb and raised him from the dead continued to spread the word. Many people, because they had heard that he had given this miraculous sign, went out to meet him. So the Pharisees said to one another, "See, this is getting us nowhere. Look how the whole world has gone after him!" (John 12:17-19)

The Pharisees could tell modern unbelievers a great deal about Jesus. They would have to admit that he raised the dead, that he healed the blind, that he opened the ears of the deaf, that he fed thousands of people by miracle, that he stilled the storm with a command. They can also testify to the fact that he set their guards back on their heels:

> Finally the temple guards went back to the chief priests and Pharisees, who asked them, "Why didn't you bring him in?" "No one ever spoke the way this man does," the guards declared. "You mean he has deceived you also?" the Pharisees retorted. (John 7:45-47)

And they can testify to the fact that he knew the meaning of their Bible better than they did! He continually embarrassed them by showing the crowd the real meaning of Scripture, which contradicted the Pharisees' interpretation:

Are you not in error because you do not know the Scriptures or the power of God? (Mark 12:24)

Now we can't ignore their testimony. They themselves admitted that they were up against a power and wisdom here that they couldn't reckon with.

If such avowed enemies of Christ had to admit that he was what he claimed to be, and that he did do what the Gospel writers wrote about him, no modern skeptic has the right to doubt the Gospel record. The Pharisees would have to (unwillingly, to be sure) silence the skeptic and assure him that all that was said about Jesus is definitely true.

Jonah: It may be a surprise to you that a prophet of Israel was a hostile witness! Supposedly he would be on God's side; God calls his Prophets to testify to the reality of spiritual matters as friendly witnesses, people who are committed to building up and looking forward to the coming Kingdom.

But God called Jonah to preach repentance to the Ninevites, and to Jonah that was one of the worst jobs he could have been assigned to! He hated the Ninevites; they were Israel's enemy. As far as he was concerned, God should just go ahead and destroy those people.

So when God called Jonah to travel to Nineveh and preach to them, he tried going in the opposite direction. He didn't get very far: God sent a "great fish" that swallowed Jonah, teaching the prophet that nobody can get away from God or shirk the responsibility that God gives him.

So Jonah went to Nineveh and preached the necessity of repentance. No doubt he was hoping that the people of that city would ignore his message and bring down on their heads a just punishment. But his hopes were dashed: the people believed his message, were terrified of this God who threatened destruction, and showed obvious and immediate signs of a true, heart-felt repentance.

Jonah was disgusted. He went up on a hill overlooking the city and sulked. God spoke to him there, and what the prophet says to God reveals the shattering revelation of God that he was struggling with:

> But Jonah was greatly displeased and became angry. He prayed to the LORD, "O LORD, is this not what I said when I was still at home? That is why I was so quick to flee to Tarshish. I knew that you are *a gracious and compassionate God, slow to anger and abounding in love*, a God who relents from sending calamity. Now, O LORD, take away my life, for it is better for me to die than to live." (Jonah 4:1-3)

That phrase "a gracious and compassionate God, slow to anger and abounding in love" is from Exodus 34:6, a famous formula that defines the special name that Israel's God claimed for himself. Jonah may or may not have thought seriously about that formula in the past, but now he was face to face with the reality of the Lord – that God really was a compassionate and gracious God. So compassionate and gracious, in fact, that he will freely forgive a pagan people whom Jonah thought had no right to forgiveness.

Jonah couldn't deny what had happened, and being a prophet he knew very well the staggering implications of what had just happened to the people of Nineveh. If God would do such a thing as this, he could extend his mercy to *anybody* around the globe. The Jewish pride of "we're the only ones whom God loves" was shattered that day.

Egyptians: When God sent Moses to Pharaoh in Egypt, the message was this: let my people go! And to the mighty Pharaoh, this was a ridiculous demand. He was certainly not about to let millions of state-owned slaves just pick up and leave the country! And he knew that he had the power to keep them there, and perhaps the legal right – since all these people were born in Egypt, under Egyptian rule.

But he didn't reckon on the power of Israel's God. In a series of miracles, God pulverized Egypt into submission. He sent plague after plague upon Pharaoh's nation, and at the same time preserved his own people from the destruction even though they lived in the same area. Pharaoh saw for himself what Moses' God could do, and his own gods couldn't keep up. Several times he admitted that he was up against a power that he couldn't deal with, but at the last minute he always backed out and refused to grant Moses' request.

The tenth plague broke Egypt's back. When God put to death all the first-born of Egypt's families, from Pharaoh's on down – and yet preserved, again, all of Israel's first-born – Pharaoh finally surrendered.

> During the night Pharaoh summoned Moses and Aaron and said, "Up! Leave my people, you and the Israelites! Go, worship the LORD as you have requested. Take your flocks and herds, as you have said, and go. And also bless me." (Exodus 12:31-32)

The country lay in ruins, all the crops were destroyed, the livestock were slaughtered, and now the dead of his people covered the entire land. Pharaoh was forced to admit that not only was Israel's God powerful, but anybody who was foolish enough to go into battle with this God will most certainly lose.

Yet Pharaoh wasn't ready to give up! He sent his army chasing the Israelites after they left, and the army caught up with them at the Red Sea. Seemingly the Israelites were helpless sheep caught between the wolf and disaster! But in one parting shot, God totally destroyed Pharaoh's army while preserving and delivering his people. So once again the pagan is forced to admit that he lost against a God that he severely underestimated.

Sodom & Gomorra: Perhaps no cities in history have experienced such an awesome display of firepower from Heaven as Sodom and Gomorra! It was so sudden and thoroughly destructive that we can liken it to an atomic blast. The cities were destroyed completely, with no trace left, *without* a bomb – with fire from Heaven. Such an act was the judgment and power of God.

The Sodomites were an object lesson. They were so perverted, so reprobate, that God was disgusted with them. Their reputation for perversion was widespread over the civilized world. But as in our day, most people just shrugged their shoulders and figured that it couldn't be helped, the Sodomites were going to do what they wanted and that was that.

What the Sodomites (or anybody else, for that matter) failed to reckon with was the holiness of God. God isn't content with sinners' lifestyles, nor does he take the philosophical approach to sin that we do. He plans wrath and destruction against sinners. While we may want to shrug at sin and put up with it, God will *never* put up with it. There will eventually be a day when all sin, even what was done in the past, will be accounted for – will be thoroughly paid for.

The question is this: is God so willing to punish sinners that he would completely destroy them? This isn't an academic question. We need to know this, because if he is then we must do whatever we can to turn away from sin before he destroys *us*. And that's what the story of Sodom and Gomorrah is designed to teach us.

As you know, God does destroy the wicked. He gave them the chance to repent – he sent in angels ahead of time, and with Lot they pleaded with the Sodomites to turn from their filthy lives. But they didn't even find ten righteous men in the city. In God's eyes, the people of Sodom deserved to die. And that's what they experienced. We can argue about it all we want, but the Sodomites can testify to us that God does in fact destroy the reprobate. There's no argument against the facts.

The rich man: Jesus told the story about the rich man and Lazarus, and some have wondered whether it was just a story or an account about real people. But the point is that such a thing happens all the time; it really doesn't change a thing if the rich man was a symbol to illustrate a point, because there are millions of souls who now find themselves in the situation that he did.

The rich man didn't give the God of Israel a serious thought in his entire life. When he died, however, he discovered that God *is* real, and that his threats of Hell *are* real. He was amazed by the wrath of God! He may have had arguments against Hell in his lifetime (as many do now) but there was no denying it when he found himself there.

The only thought on his mind when he was there suffering in eternal punishment was to try to get to his family and warn them about Hell:

> Then I beg you, father, send Lazarus to my father's house, for I have five brothers. Let him warn them, so that they will not also come to this place of torment. (Luke 16:27-28)

This is an amazing admission from a formerly hardened, unbelieving, rebellious sinner. He wasn't in denial anymore. He in fact *wanted* to testify to – be a witness of – the reality of the Judge of Heaven, the reality and seriousness of sin, the fires of Hell, the sufferings of the damned, and God's final refusal for any drop of mercy to the condemned. If we don't accept his testimony of what he himself experienced, we probably won't take *anybody* seriously.

Made to order

One sobering truth about the wicked is that God has made plans for them. They no doubt thought that they could avoid God completely, that if they ignored him then he would ignore them. They will soon learn what a mistake that is.

God hand-picks his witnesses, because it's crucial that he gets the glory he deserves and that he achieves his goals in history. He picked the Prophets and the Apostles and trained them in his ways; their testimony is critical for the life and growth of the Church. But he also picked some of the wicked to witness his works. The Lord particularly wanted people who were in well-placed positions in history, and people who hated or despised him and his people. If *these* people saw God, others in history would be more impressed by their testimony than an account from someone with no importance.

So God set up the situation for the greatest effect. He carefully chose the time and place as well as the people involved.

> ... But the Lord laughs at the wicked, for he knows their day is coming. (Psalm 37:13)

> The LORD works out everything for his own ends – even the wicked for a day of disaster. (Proverbs 16:4)

> The Lord knows how to rescue godly men from trials and to hold the unrighteous for the day of judgment, while continuing their punishment. This is especially true of those who follow the corrupt desire of the sinful nature and despise authority. (2 Peter 2:9-10)

The point is that, unknown to them, and certainly against their wishes, God is using the wicked for his own ends. They are being cornered into being God's "employees," so to speak – they work for him and help him achieve his goals. They of course would rather be left alone (so that they can continue to undermine the work of God!). But his wisdom and ways are so far above the puny mind of man that he can easily manipulate man's affairs to his own purposes.

> In his heart a man plans his course, but the LORD determines his steps. (Proverbs 16:19)

> Many are the plans in a man's heart, but it is the LORD's purpose that prevails. (Proverbs 19:21)

On the last day there will be a gigantic trial in Heaven, and everyone who ever lived will be there as defendants. The righteous are expecting to be justified and let into their eternal reward. But the wicked have double reason to fear that day. *First*, God will show everyone the sin and unbelief and rebellion in their hearts, to the extent that his sentence of doom will be seen to be entirely just and appropriate.

Second, they will be forced to glorify God on that day. That's the last thing they want to do, certainly, but they won't be able to stop themselves. God will use them to display his infinite wisdom, his power, his justice, and his holiness. Their entire lives will be a testimony of the battle against good and evil: they will be shown for what they are, as they stand there in front of the God they've tried to defy all their lives yet finally lost to.

The Witness of the Church

Usually when we think of a witness we think of someone using modern evangelistic methods to spread the Gospel of Christ to an unbelieving world. But if we aren't careful, we can actually water the idea down so much that it loses its original power and meaning. "Witnessing" is not what many modern Christians think it is.

We have already seen that a witness is someone who has seen God – and he can tell us what he experienced in that encounter. That in itself is a simple idea. But modern evangelical "witnesses" end up doing a great deal of teaching and preaching instead of talking about a personal experience of God. Because of this confusion, the act of witnessing has actually become something different than its original Biblical form. This is, perhaps, one of the reasons for the frustrating failure of the modern Church to make a significant impact on our culture. Unbelievers just aren't impressed with our doctrine anymore, because they don't see our God anymore.

We have a problem

There does seem to be something wrong with modern day evangelism. There are more people out witnessing on our streets today than there ever have been in history. And they will end up saying just about anything – right or wrong! – as they plead, threaten, beg, or bribe people to believe in Jesus! What some people end up saying about God is, unfortunately, very dishonoring to him. Modern evangelicals often add things to the Gospel, supposedly to make it a bit sweeter to swallow; but that takes away from the Gospel instead of enhances it. It's no wonder that an astute unbeliever looks at today's evangelists as not much more credible than a shady used-car salesman.

Another sign that things aren't right is that, especially in mass meetings, thousands will turn to the Gospel and "believe in Jesus." But Jesus said that *very few* will enter the narrow gate to eternal life; did he know what he was talking about? We know that most of these revival "conversions" aren't genuine. Studies have been done with people who have made professions of faith in revival meetings; and, after a few years, most of them have fallen away from Christ. Again, Jesus anticipated this when he taught about the seed falling on stony and thorny ground.

> The one who received the seed that fell on rocky places is the man who hears the word and at once receives it with joy. But since he has no root, he lasts only a short time. When trouble or persecution comes because of the word, he quickly falls away. The one who received the seed that fell among the thorns is the man who hears the word, but the worries of this life and the deceitfulness of wealth choke it, making it unfruitful. (Matthew 13:20-22)

A third symptom of our methods of evangelization is that the "new life" that people claim to have found in Christ has little effect on their lives. There have been studies done on Christians in churches and their attitudes on fundamentals of the faith. For example, 53% of evangelical Christians claim that there is "no such thing as absolute truth." (What happened to the Bible?) It gets even worse: 56% of "fundamentalist" singles engage in sex outside of marriage; 49% believe in the right to abort one's baby; and 49% believe in euthanasia – the killing of the aged and infirm.[2] Something is wrong here. It's getting increasingly difficult to single out the Christians in our society: they live in the same way, and hold to the same world-view, as their unbelieving neighbors. This most definitely is not the advice that Paul gave us!

---

[2] Veith, Gene Edward, *Postmodern Times*, 1994 Crossway Books; pp.16-18.

> So I tell you this, and insist on it in the Lord, that you must no longer live as the Gentiles do, in the futility of their thinking. They are darkened in their understanding and separated from the life of God because of the ignorance that is in them due to the hardening of their hearts. Having lost all sensitivity, they have given themselves over to sensuality so as to indulge in every kind of impurity, with a continual lust for more.
>
> You, however, did not come to know Christ that way. Surely you heard of him and were taught in him in accordance with the truth that is in Jesus. You were taught, with regard to your former way of life, to put off your old self, which is being corrupted by its deceitful desires; to be made new in the attitude of your minds; and to put on the new self, created to be like God in true righteousness and holiness. (Ephesians 4:17-24)

It's time to take a hard look at the so-called converts to Christianity. Obviously if there's no change of heart, if people end up believing the wrong things about God and themselves, and they continue to live in what the Bible says is sin, then the "witness" didn't do his or her job. It's time to go back to the basics and find out exactly what "witnessing" is.

The trick is to use what we've already learned. We've looked carefully at what the Bible says about witnesses, and we've found the same theme running across all the examples. It doesn't make sense to throw all that information away and make up a new method that suits our modern church. God expects us to study his Word and find out how to do things *his* way. As we do that, we become proficient in his work and get results that please him, not ourselves. "Do your best to present yourself to God as one approved, a workman who does not need to be ashamed and who correctly handles the word of truth." (2 Timothy 2:15)

A derived witness

First things first. We must never forget our roots: we have what we have, and we know what we know, only because of the witnesses who came before us. We can't move away from the foundation that the Prophets and Apostles laid down for us. If our testimony differs from theirs in any way, then we are outside of the truth and can't claim God's blessing or protection on our work.

The testimony of the Prophets and Apostles are crucial for the life of the entire Church – including for our day. *They* heard God; *they* watched God at work. At *that* stage of history, God was teaching his people what he was really like. And his witnesses wrote all of this down so that the rest of the people of God would always know what God is like. Who of us can contradict what they saw? Can we throw out their testimony and replace it with our own? We weren't there! God made sure that we would get the *facts* about him through his Prophets and Apostles. Nobody can change that truth now.

> Consequently, you are no longer foreigners and aliens, but fellow citizens with God's people and members of God's household, built on the foundation of the Apostles and Prophets, with Christ Jesus himself as the chief cornerstone. (Ephesians 2:19-20)

It also means that we must put every experience that we have to a ruthless test: is this, in fact, *God* talking to us? We claim that we have experienced God in our lives; but compare what God did and said with what the Bible teaches about how God works. Does your experience match the Biblical model? If not, then how do you know for sure that it was the God of the Bible that you were dealing with? Remember that we have the testimony of the Prophets and Apostles that *this* is the way God works! Can we contradict their testimony? I know that it's unthinkable, but there are many other gods – devils, that is – and followers of those gods who would love to deceive us about spiritual matters.

For such men are false apostles, deceitful workmen, masquerading as apostles of Christ. And no wonder, for Satan himself masquerades as an angel of light. It is not surprising, then, if his servants masquerade as servants of righteousness. (2 Corinthians 11:13-15)

Our faith, if it's genuine, proves that the testimony of the Apostles was true. What the Bible says happens at conversion, really does happen. The God of the Bible comes into our lives and does the kinds of things that we read about in the Bible.

The world often hears about Christ and the Gospel, but their most often-heard comment is this: show me someone who *lives* it. They love to tear down the Church because of the hypocrisy and sins of Christians who are supposed to be following Jesus. Though it's irrational to deny Christ because of the sins of his followers, unbelievers still have a point which God intends to address. Our witness has to be about a reality: a changed heart, a new life, separation from the old life, new emotions and likes and dislikes. Though the truth of God is still true even if we mess up our own lives, sin contradicts our witness and gives the unbeliever a reason to think that we don't really believe in God ourselves. Righteousness, however, which comes through faith in Christ, speaks volumes about the reality of God and is hard for a sinner to argue against.

When Christ truly saves a person, that person's life changes completely. He has a new heart full of the life of Christ, he hates sin, he loves God and holiness, he loves his neighbor and his enemy, he lives for the Heavenly kingdom instead of this world, he starts working on the spiritual kingdom. This is hard to account for except as proof that the testimony of the Bible is true – that God is real, and this happens to a person who meets God. Paul loved to see it happen; it was proof again and again of the truth of his Gospel:

For what is our hope, our joy, or the crown in which we will glory in the presence of our Lord Jesus when he comes? Is it not you? Indeed, you are our glory and joy. (1 Thessalonians 2:19-20)

It's encouraging to the saints, and unnerving to the world, to see those "old" truths appear again in our generation. Just when our society thought it had buried old-fashioned morality forever, a new movement starts in the Church: people who hear the Law of God and cry out to him in remorse and repentance for the sins that they committed against him. Just when science "proves" that miracles don't happen anymore, a thoroughly wicked man or woman completely changes overnight into a child of God, pulled out of darkness into light – and walks the rest of their days in holiness. Just when our educational and political systems thought that they had successfully indoctrinated all of us in their world view, now there are people who despise this world, sell all that they have, and turn their thoughts to God's kingdom instead. Over and over the old Biblical themes are appearing again in our day, proving the skeptics wrong about the ancient witness of the Prophets and Apostles. God still lives among his people!

Depending on the Spirit's testimony

We belong to a long chain of witnesses that starts at the very beginning of the Bible. The Spirit's work in us is to bring us close to the same God who first revealed himself to the Prophets: to Moses, to Abraham, to the Apostles. And the purpose of *our* testimony is also to show the world that God is real. God really does do the same things that we read about in his Word! We are living proof that Jesus Christ still lives and works among his people, doing the same kinds of things and working on the same Kingdom that he came to set up originally. We are the later generation of a long, continuous history; we are part of the same living Church that the Apostles were part of.

Our role as witnesses is extremely important, because we are "living letters" that show the reality of God's spiritual world.

> You yourselves are our letter, written on our hearts, known and read by everybody. You show that you are a letter from Christ, the result of our ministry, written not with ink but with the Spirit of the living

God, not on tablets of stone but on tablets of human hearts. (2 Corinthians 3:2-3)

If we are this important to the growth of the Kingdom of God, you can be sure that the Spirit is going to involve himself heavily in our witnessing. We've already seen that in order to be a true witness of God, someone has to get his information through the Spirit – who is the source of all information about God. And the Spirit starts with the Word of God: he teaches us God's truth and opens our spiritual eyes to see the reality of God's world. Then he empowers us to take hold of what we see, and live by faith in Christ who provides what our souls need. At every step of the way, the Spirit is making it possible for us to live in the reality of Heaven. When it comes time to tell others of what God has done, then, our testimony will be based on the careful work of the Spirit in our hearts.

This is how the Spirit makes our testimony powerful and effective. Many people think that the Spirit is going to make us say ecstatic things, utter prophecies, and perform other mysterious acts that we sometimes find in the Old Testament stories of Spirit-filled prophets. Actually it's a much quieter affair and much more impressive to unbelievers. If we danced around strangely in front of them, they wouldn't understand what is going on and would probably reject us. But when we tell them of what the Spirit has already done in our hearts – and have the evidence to back up our claims (which includes peace, joy, purity, forgiveness, strength, love, gentleness, self-control) – then people see something real and useful. They can see that God has been saving you, not just making you look ridiculous.

What is the purpose of the Church?

The Church is specially designed to witness about God. It's a shame that the modern Church has forgotten this very important point. Too often when we walk into a church, what we see is lots of man – his works, his glory, his holiness. But how can someone be saved unless they see God? And where are they going to see him if not in the body of Christ where God lives?

If you want to see a graphic example of what I mean, look at the hymns that you sing in your church service. Almost all of them are a wonderful display of the nature and works of God. Hymns tell about what God has done. They focus on him; they only bring man into the picture to show how we should relate to this very special God.

The rest of the worship service should also be totally focused on God. But even though the Bible is read, and prayers are made, we too often look at ourselves in the service: what *we* should be like, what *we* should do, what *we* ought not to do, the faith and patience and love that *we* should have. After most church services, we come away feeling that we've heard very little about God and a lot about our own responsibilities.

This is backwards. The only way we can know what our responsibilities are is to first get in touch with the King. Knowing who he is will greatly affect what we have to be and do. We only find out who we are by being in his presence.

The apostolic writers understood this point well. Paul, for example, focused on something about God and Christ at least 100 times in his short letter to the Ephesians! It's about as long as an average sermon would be; but he obviously felt it was important to make God the subject of his letter.

Sermons and Sunday School lessons need to be about God. The Church exists to hold *Jesus* up for all to see, not man. We are to testify about the Lord, and tell the world what he is and does. Unless we do that, we can't count on seeing many conversions, and we certainly won't see much spiritual growth in the churches. We can't grow on information about ourselves; we have to be fed the Bread from Heaven if we're going to grow. God is the Savior; we need to get in touch with him. And that contact has to be real and vital, not just dropping his Name around in the service. As the sons of Sceva discovered, throwing God's name around can really backfire on us if we don't know what we're doing! (Acts 19:13-16)

Not every Christian is called to be an evangelist. In the list of spiritual gifts that Paul gave us, those people who evangelize, or spread the Gospel, are *one* of many kinds of workers in Christ's Church – others being teachers, preachers, those who do good deeds, those who encourage, and so on. But we are *all* called to testify to what God has done for us:

> Always be prepared to give an answer to everyone who asks you to give the reason for the hope that you have. (1 Peter 3:15)

If we are Christians, if we are the children of God, then we do have a hope in Christ – and that makes us live differently from others. If our lives are centered on God, if we get everything from God and trust in him for everything, if we walk with God daily and grow constantly in the knowledge of God, then we have something definite to say to the world about God. We can't miss this golden opportunity to point the world to him who loves us so much. Unbelievers are going to want to know the reason for a life of joy, stability, holiness and peace. And, when they ask us about it, that's the opportunity that we're looking for to testify to them about what God has done.

The difference between witnessing and teaching

Modern evangelism is often confused with teaching and preaching. In fact, we can best see this problem in the way new converts are encouraged to go out in the streets and "spread the Gospel." What they end up doing is trying to preach some doctrine – often the "Four Spiritual Laws" – and getting their potential convert to agree to the truth of that doctrine. This isn't being a witness.

The weakness behind sending people out with doctrine is that often they run into people's strange ideas that they've never heard before, and they don't know what to do with that. If your potential convert is a member of another denomination, or a cult, for example, they can easily throw you a problem that will only confuse the conversation. They may have difficult questions about your faith that they want to know about. If you're not careful, you can easily get caught up in an argument (and many times those arguments will only hurt your chances of getting them to listen to you) instead of sharing the Gospel. This happens too often.

Only a person who has studied the Bible and Christian doctrine to a great extent is capable of handling most situations like that. They can usually clear up and disentangle a person's wrong perceptions about Christianity, and steer them into the truth that they need to hear. But unless you are very familiar with the Bible's teachings, the best course of action is to not walk into an argument in the first place. Instead, you ought to get good at giving your personal testimony.

Testimony is simply telling people what God did for you. It's such a simple approach that we often miss its amazing power. If God really did something for you in your life, something concrete that's easily seen and understood, there is no way that someone can deny that. They would have to call you a liar! And without evidence or eyewitness testimony to the contrary, the only option they have is to believe you.

You would be amazed at the difference in the two approaches. Trying to talk someone into believing doctrine about God will usually get you nowhere; everyone has their own opinions on what God is, and they will most likely fight you about the issue. But telling them about a concrete answer to prayer, for example, or getting free from a sin, or the peace and knowledge that comes from the Spirit, or the wonderful enlightenment that comes from a Bible verse, is an unanswerable argument. You will find them interested and eager to hear what you have to say. They want this too! They wish that their god were as alive and real as your God seems to be.

What you're doing by testifying to God's works in your life is challenging them to produce a real God of their own. They can't. Their god doesn't exist; their god doesn't answer prayer. When you can demonstrate the reality of your God, however, they not only can't refute what you say, it will most likely make them interested in switching Gods. You are really using a weapon they don't have, in order to capture the enemy's slaves for the Kingdom of God. Show them a God they really want, and they will let you lead them to him.

Levels of testimony

Our aim is to continue the chain of testimony of the reality of God. It started a long time ago, with Abraham and the covenant that God made with him and his descendants. It continued through the history of the Jews, and culminated in the ministry of Christ and the Apostles. All of these witnesses saw or heard God, and testified to his works. But lest the world think that God's work is over, the Lord *continues* the process in us. We now testify that the God of our fathers is still alive and does the same kinds of work among men and women.

The Church was specially designed to testify to the reality of God. Certain things happen in the Church that can't be accounted for in any other way:

- *Worship* – There are all kinds of practices that fall under the label "worship," but really the focus of our worship is supposed to be God himself. We aren't gathered together to think about us, but about him.

    Jesus promised that "where two or three come together in my name, there am I with them." (Matthew 18:20) This is unique among all the religions of the world! Our God comes among us; he's within our reach, so that we can see him and know him. This happens because of the Spirit, of course, who brings us into the presence of God.

    So it's especially important to do things in the worship service that draw our attention to God. Who is he? What has he done? What does he like and not like? What does he do for his people? Why should we fear him? These are the kinds of things that come out when people approach him in person. When we see him like this, we are encouraged to keep trusting him, to keep fearing him and obeying his commands. Others, when they join us in our worship, will see God as a result of our worship and be amazed at how real he is:

> But if an unbeliever or someone who does not understand comes in while everybody is prophesying, he will be convinced by all that he is a sinner and will be judged by all, and the secrets of his heart will be laid bare. So he will fall down and worship God, exclaiming, "God is really among you!" (1 Corinthians 14:24-25)

- *Conversions* – The way that the Church grows is through more people coming into the Church. But the Church isn't like other social groups. Our membership consists of changed people, people who were once in darkness and now they see the light. They knew almost nothing about God; he was just a rumor to them, or a tradition. But now they have seen him and know him. Christians have been "born again" spiritually so that they can live in the light of Heaven.

Take Paul for an example. For his entire life he was a Jew, a Pharisee, a student of the Law and zealous for the traditions of the Jews. He was so intent on preserving the traditions that he persecuted Christians who were upsetting everyone with their new religion. Suddenly a light shines out of Heaven, he falls to the ground, and in an instant he becomes a different person. He no longer persecutes the Christians – he helps them! He became the greatest of the Apostles and the most capable teacher of the great mysteries of the Gospel that the Church ever had.

How do you account for such a change? Obviously it wasn't from anything in himself, or his training. We simply have to accept his account of the matter – he gave us a testimony of what Christ did to him on that day (see Acts 22 and 26). So it is with all of God's people. They have been touched by God, and now they are new creatures. Their testimony reveals how that happened.

- *Condemning the world* – Christians have been changed for a reason. They used to be like everyone else in the world – ignorant, rebellious, wicked, miserable, and headed for death.

> As for you, you were dead in your transgressions and sins, in which you used to live when you followed the ways of this world and of the ruler of the kingdom of the air, the spirit who is now at work in those who are disobedient. All of us also lived among them at one time, gratifying the cravings of our sinful nature and following its desires and thoughts. Like the rest, we were by nature objects of wrath. (Ephesians 2:1-3)

God lifted us up in Christ to live a new life – of righteousness, peace, and joy in the Holy Spirit. Now we look different from others who haven't been saved from sin (or at least we gradually do – it takes time!). The result is that the world isn't going to like us anymore. In fact, they will quickly grow to hate us.

We now love what they hate; and we now hate what they still love. We have nothing in common with them. They are willingly headed away from God and to destruction; we are, with all our heart, headed to Heaven and Christ.

> Do not be yoked together with unbelievers. For what do righteousness and wickedness have in common? Or what fellowship can light have

with darkness? What harmony is there between Christ and Belial? What does a believer have in common with an unbeliever? What agreement is there between the temple of God and idols? For we are the temple of the living God. As God has said: "I will live with them and walk among them, and I will be their God, and they will be my people." "Therefore come out from them and be separate, says the Lord. Touch no unclean thing, and I will receive you." "I will be a Father to you, and you will be my sons and daughters, says the Lord Almighty." (1 Corinthians 6:14-18)

Furthermore, this won't be a hard thing for us to do. Unbelievers don't like to be around us! They will drift away on their own, because the smell of life is too much for them. The unfortunate thing is when they decide that they would rather be rid of you – and they start making trouble for you. Persecution is inevitable for the people of God, and it's all because you are a living condemnation of the lifestyle of unbelievers and their state of heart. Your righteousness testifies to them that God is *holy* – because God is making you holy.

Who can testify to what?

Let's not be confused about this issue. Most of today's "witnessing" is actually forms of teaching and preaching, and that's a mistake. For some reason we like to send new-born Christians out on the street to "witness" to strangers, when what we are really asking them to do is *teach* about Christianity – when they don't even know the basics of the faith yet! Some people are gifted at teaching and preaching, but not everyone is.

Actually every Christian can testify about God. If we stick to our original definition, every Christian should be living in the presence of God, so that he or she has something to tell others about what is happening spiritually in their lives. *That's* witnessing!

The **spiritually newborn** can testify to what God has done in their hearts – he woke them up, he called them by name, he forgave their sins, he filled their hearts with peace and joy, he showed them their savior in Jesus, he gave them hope of Heaven, he gave them a love for his Word.

The **martyrs** of the Church, those who are called to suffer persecution and death for his name's sake, can testify to what God has done in their hearts – he filled their eyes and hearts with the vision of Heaven, he gave them strength to suffer whatever their enemies inflicted on them, he encouraged them to despise the world and reach out for the life in Christ waiting for them in Heaven.

The **teachers and preachers** in the Church can testify to what God has done in their hearts – he revealed his precious truths to them in his Word, he gave them boldness and the spiritual skill to make Christ plain to their hearers, he gave them fruit from their ministry as many people hear the Word and believe in the God they testify to.

The **encouragers** of the Church can testify to what God has done in their hearts – he comforted them in their trials (2 Corinthians 1:3-7), he showed them the riches in Christ that is theirs, he led them to the right people who needed that same word of encouragement.

A bold witness

There is one more point to remember as you fulfill your calling as God's witness. Having experienced the reality of God, you *know* that what you testify about him is true. There's no doubt about it. So declare it boldly to the world! Don't be afraid, don't beg for a hearing or plead with them to accept what you are saying. Don't bother to dress it up in academic language to make it go down easier for rebellious unbelievers. You have the words of life; they are dead, and they desperately need this news from Heaven. You can see; they can't. So declare it confidently, boldly, clearly, so that they can understand you easily. You don't need to be obnoxious about it – if there is to be any offense, they should be offended with what they hear about God, not with the way you witness to them. Your message is about God, not yourself! Nevertheless, God's people have a life-giving message for a dying world: God is real, Jesus is alive, and there is salvation for all who believe and repent and come to Christ for forgiveness.

> "You are my witnesses," declares the LORD, "and my servant whom I have chosen, so that you may know and believe me and understand that I am he. Before me no god was formed, nor will there be one after me. I, even I, am the LORD, and apart from me there is no savior. I have revealed and saved and proclaimed – I, and not some foreign god among you. You are my witnesses," declares the LORD, "that I am God. Yes, and from ancient days I am he. No one can deliver out of my hand. When I act, who can reverse it?" (Isaiah 43:10-13)

Remember Jesus' warning:

> If anyone is ashamed of me and my words, the Son of Man will be ashamed of him when he comes in his glory and in the glory of the Father and of the holy angels. (Luke 9:26)

If we hold back, if we are ashamed of these spiritual realities, then we put a bad light on the things of God before the world. It makes it look as if we have our own doubts about whether he is real! Instead, we need the Spirit of Paul –

> Pray also for me, that whenever I open my mouth, words may be given me so that I will fearlessly make known the mystery of the gospel, for which I am an

ambassador in chains. Pray that I may declare it fearlessly, as I should. (Ephesians 6:19-20)

Conclusion

Hopefully you can see now that the entire Bible is God's strategy of using the testimony of eyewitnesses. There are many kinds of witnesses, but we can't dismiss what they say without calling them liars. And in a court of law, if you don't want to believe the testimony of the witness, that means you have to provide your own witnesses who can prove that the testimony is a lie. In the case of the Bible's witnesses, we have no hope of doing that.

This means that the Bible's testimony is rock-solid. It's compelling proof that we're dealing with the truth in this book. We simply have no recourse but to believe it. On Judgment Day we will find out, if we haven't learned before then, how necessary the Bible's testimony is for our salvation. It would be wise for us to listen and learn now before that day comes. This is, after all, why God resorted to this strategy. Our faith *must* rest on solid testimony so that we know we have a real salvation and a real God to believe in. There was no other way to achieve God's purpose of our salvation but to amass this wealth of testimony.

The purpose of the Bible's witnesses, remember, is to prove to us that *there really is a God*, and *he's really like what the Bible says about him*. As we learn to shed our wrong notions about God, and take seriously this testimony to his nature and works, then we too will experience the reality of this God. Then we too will have a testimony about him to share with the world.

www.ingramcontent.com/pod-product-compliance
Lightning Source LLC
Chambersburg PA
CBHW022004160426
43197CB00007B/261